ABOUT THE AUTHOR

Poe Ballantine currently lives in Chadron, Nebraska. He has been travelling around America for over thirty years, writing most of the time. His stories have garnered a number of nominations and awards, including the Best American Short Story Award in 1998. He is the author of two novels and two books of non-fiction, all of which will be published by Old Street.

Also by Poe Ballantine:

God Clobbers Us All
Decline and Fall of the Lawrence Welk Empire
501 Minutes to Christ

THINGS I LIKE ABOUT AMERICA

POE

BALLANTINE

THINGS I LIKE ABOUT AMERICA

POE BALLANTINE

Old St PUBLISHING

First published 2002 by Hawthorne Books & Literary Arts, Oregon USA

First published in Great Britain in 2009 by Old Street Publishing Ltd

This edition published 2009 by Old Street Publishing Ltd
40 Bowling Green Lane, London EC1R 0NE
www.oldstreetpublishing.co.uk

ISBN 978-1-906964-06-1

Typeset by Old Street Publishing.
Printed and bound in Great Britain by J F Print, Ltd.

This book is for my two favorite people in the world, my mother and father.

Acknowledgments

NATURALLY, I WOULD LIKE TO THANK THE GOOGENBERRY Foundation, the Harry Paratestes Trust, and the Ugly French Motor-scooter Club, but my real gratitude goes out to the editorial staff of *The Sun*: Sy Safransky, Andrew Snee, Colleen Donfield, Seth Mirsky and Julia Burke, who believed in me from the beginning and without whose help I would almost certainly still be lost among the horticultural exhibits at the county fair.

Contents

She's Got Barney Rubble Eyes

I GRADUATED FROM HIGH SCHOOL WHEN I WAS SEVENTEEN AND immediately moved out of my parents' house into a two-bedroom apartment on Central Avenue in East San Diego with my best friend, Dewy Daldorph, who had recently become a devout Christian. Dewy quickly grew tired of my secular and festive exploits (and my inability to see the light) and moved into a little hut by himself on Redondo Court in Mission Beach, where he could spend more intimate time with his Nazarene girlfriend, though it turned out that she hated the beach. I couldn't afford the rent, so my two good high school buddies Woodchuck and Goldie moved in with me and shared a room. Woodchuck had a job as a parts delivery driver and Goldie, my second best friend, named for his prominent gold front tooth, was welding iron grillwork in Old Town. We filled the place with bong smoke and beer cans and dreams of beautiful or even passably attractive or even, after seven or eight bongs and a dozen cans of beer, two-legged women, while *Dark Side of the Moon* played over and over on the little Panasonic stereo by the window.

I was working full time at Pine Manor Convalescent Hospital downtown, which was packed with attractive young women in short nylon dresses. I joked with them and stared at them and imagined that I could skillfully conceal my erections. Then, one day, I was headed down the hospital corridor about to turn the corner into the break room when I heard what sounded like a donkey being dragged by a tugboat into a river. A new aide in crisp whites sat at a table, her mouth open, the tormented braying sounds emanating thence. Someone, perhaps she, had apparently told a joke. She was laughing all by herself. Her mouth snapped shut when she saw me, and she stared at me as I if were a stuffed duckling dinner with dumplings and buttered baby carrots. No one had ever stared at me like this before. I was a skinny drip with pimples and glasses. Her eyes looked funny and I thought she must be nearsighted. I felt so buffoonishly unnerved and stick-figured and cranberry-faced with sudden prickly rash in my shorts that I moved straight to the snack machine and pretended that she did not exist.

Later that evening she came over to my section, stuck her head in the room where I was working, and smiled at me. 'Hi there,' she said.

'Hi.'

'I was wondering if you could help me.'

'What is it?'

'I've gotta lift up old Mrs. Fatface, or whatever her name is. In 213.'

'Mrs. Ferris.'

'Yeah, whatever.' She tipped her head and threw back her long, tawny, center-parted, dyed-from-brunette hair. 'I need some help.'

'OK,' I said. I followed her down the hall. She moved gracelessly with a mince in her step like an arthritic geisha or a grenade victim from a foreign war.

'My name's Bonnie Newton,' she said, turning her head and opening her pale, masculine mouth at me.

I introduced myself, making sure not to shake her hand because I had recently read a magazine article that stated if you wanted to sleep with a woman, never shake her hand.

'Why don't we take a break?' said Bonnie, after we had taken care of Mrs. Ferris. 'You up for a break?'

She smoked True 100's, plastic-filtered cigarettes with so little tar and nicotine in them it made you wonder what was the point of smoking them. I smoked Marlboro reds in the box. We were all alone in the break room with the Pepsi machine humming. Her weird, fuzzy eyes were like puddles of shoe polish, and the sharply arched eyebrows above them were darker and more unnatural still, as if she had plucked them completely out, dyed the hairs individually the blackest, most raven black, then replaced each one, inserting the follicles into the pores with a good eyebrow glue. I couldn't think of anything to say. She leaned over and delivered a chilly scrotum-shrinking whisper in my ear: 'I don't want you to think I'm just a nurse's aide,' she said.

'What are you?'

'I'm an actress,' she said.

'Oh really. Like movies or what?'

'I'm a member of the Screen Actors Guild,' she said with a haughty jerk of the chin.

'That's great.'

'I've been involved with the Old Globe,' she added. 'And I've done some movies.'

'Really? Which ones?'

'I had a bit part when I was sixteen in *Double Damnation*. Did you see that?'

'No.'

'Jason Robards was in that, and Keenan Wynn. I got his autograph.' She nodded rapidly with a sort of squinty electrical wince. 'And I've had three auditions this year,' she continued hastily. 'And I'll be doing Old Globe Theater and summer stock starting in July, plus this guy's supposed to call me about some modeling shots.'

'Wow. You're a model too?'

'Well,' she grated in her dried-out and unmelodic voice, batting her lashes. 'It's like acting. I'd rather act, but you never know. Somebody might see the pictures or recommend me. The money's good.'

'You're sure pretty enough to be a model,' I said.

'Say,' she said. 'Why don't you come over tonight and have a glass of wine with me? Are you busy?'

'Not really.'

'I'm new in town and I haven't made any friends yet. I'll give you a ride.'

'I have a car.'

'Save the gas. I don't live far...'

Bonnie flew down A Street in the left lane in her ratty, little red canvas-top MGB. She didn't know how to drive. I wanted to grab the wheel to keep her from taking us headfirst into a bridge pillar. 'I'm superstitious!' she shouted over the Blue Öyster Cult song playing on KPRI. 'I believe that the right lane is bad luck. Are you superstitious?'

'Not too much.'

'I'm also afraid of black cats,' she shouted, tearing down the darkness of Florida Canyon and skillfully evading a crate of lettuce that had tumbled off the back of a truck. 'And nuns.'

'Nuns?' I looked back at the lettuce heads, scattered like money all over the road, with dodging headlights dancing all around them.

'I tried to be a nun once. I was too much of a rebel, though. I have a problem with authority.'

'You were in a convent?'

'That's where my modeling career started.'

'How?'

At the top of the canyon, Bonnie ran a stop sign and as my head whirled around on my neck and my fingers sank into the armrest and the onslaught of traffic converged upon us in our final seconds on earth, she explained to me

how her modeling career had begun at a nunnery. 'One
night me and five other girls sneaked out the window and
drank wine and kissed with boys from the vo-tech down
by the river. When they caught us, we had to dress this big,
dead nun for penance. She was stiff as a board, and while
we were lifting her from the table, the hoist snapped and
she sat straight up and looked at us, and we all took off out
the door. I ran away that night, hitchhiked south, and got
picked up by a guy who wanted to take pictures of me.'
She shook her head regretfully. 'My granny never forgave
me after that.'

'Why? Because you left the convent?'

'No, because she saw the *pictures*. It was a motorcycle
magazine. You know, I showed my tits. Big deal. I think she
was just jealous.' She glanced down at her prominent breasts.
They seemed like two unknown worlds to me, crying out
be explored.

'Where was this?'

'Minnesota.'

'Is that where you were born?'

'No, I was born here.'

'In San Diego?'

'My father was in the Navy.'

'You were born in Balboa Hospital?'

'I guess so. I don't remember.'

She took a left on Landis Street, roared into a lot, and
parked crookedly around the back of an apartment complex,
which, through the shaggy silver silhouettes of eucalyptus

trees, overlooked Balboa Park. I untangled myself from the
seat belt and climbed out of her death trap of a sports car.

'This is a nice-looking place,' I said.

'I was lucky to find it.'

'Where were you before?'

'Topanga Canyon. I had some work up there...'

The rank, slow perfume of potted geraniums drifted up
to my nostrils. The hairy eucalyptus trees smelled like cats
in heat. Off to the east the Romano-colored moon was
trapped behind a cloud for a moment before it finally broke
and lifted free. Bonnie led me up a flight of concrete shelf
stairs. Wind chimes tinkled and I almost kicked over a
hibachi. She stopped for a moment to jingle a key and give
the door a gentle shove, and I followed her into a hazy,
green room veiled with the smell of Charlie perfume. The
low pile carpet was chlorine blue, like a public swimming
pool. A laundry basket sat on the floor, and feminine articles
were laid over the back of the couch, pink and yellow bras,
pink and yellow panties. Two cantaloupes on her oval
dining-room table sent up a musky fragrance, like a fruity
version of the eucalyptus trees.

'Excuse the mess,' she said. 'You're my first visitor.' She
indicated the panty-decorated couch. 'Sit down.'

I took a seat amid all the heavenly underwear. On the
floor across from me was a wooden needlepoint rocking
chair and probably two hundred record albums arranged in
milk crates under an impressive NASA-black Marantz stereo.
From the opposite wall a large pastel of a woman in a broad

sun hat—a print I think everyone owned in 1973 —gazed down upon me with blithering Neil Diamond serenity.

'Why don't you take your shoes off?' she said, kicking off her own. 'I don't know how anybody can stand to wear clothes. I think deep down I'm a nudist. When I was a little girl I used to go around naked all year—even in the winter.'

'In Minnesota?'

She bent over and showed me her ample white breasts. 'Do you like apple wine?'

'Um, yeah.'

'It's Annie Green Springs. My favorite. Put on an album if you want.'

Bonnie had what I considered to be good taste in music: Led Zeppelin, Deep Purple, Neil Young, Robin Trower, the older more obscure albums of Pink Floyd, all arranged alphabetically, a good sign in a person, I decided. I extracted *Meddle* from its sleeve and set the needle in the groove.

'Good choice!' she shouted from the kitchen.

'So,' I shouted back to her. 'How did you end up at Pine Manor?'

'It was in the paper. What about you?'

I took a crotch sniff off a pair of her clean panties. 'Took a class in high school.'

'How old are you anyway?'

I cleared my throat. 'Seventeen.'

'I thought you were in your *twenties*,' she said, swinging around the corner with two glasses of wine. 'Why, you're just a baby!'

'How old are you?' I said.

'Twenty-two. That's not too old, is it? I hope you like ice.'

I thought of Woodchuck and Goldie sitting at the table smoking their bong, pining over women, and wondering where I was. They wouldn't believe it if they saw it. I took a gulp of the wine, good, cold, sweet, soda-pop wine.

We played a game of Scrabble and drank more wine. Bonnie was a poor speller and made up words: VOOGLE. I was out of Marlboros, so I smoked her True Menthol 100's, which were so low in tar and nicotine I couldn't tell if they were lit or not.

She passed me a folded note. I opened it and read: 'Sometimes I have trubble comunicating with men.'

I wrote back: 'Don't feel like you have to be nervous around me.'

'I am so happy to be with you,' she returned.

We exchanged these notes that grew increasingly strange with poor spelling, like disturbing little special education valentines.

'I'm paralized inside.'

'I have never loved,' she wrote again.

'Why don't you trust me? You think I'm going to hurt you?'

'Who am I?'

'How the hell would I know,' I wrote back. 'I just met you.'

'Men have always treated me badly,' she said, crossing her arms and staring at me with her fuzzy black eyes that were either entirely pupil or no pupil at all. By all accounts she was attractive, but whenever I looked into those eyes all I could think of was Barney Rubble.

'Well, I won't treat you badly,' I said gallantly.

'You don't have to get back right away, do you?' she said.

About one o'clock that night we drove to the 7-11 on Texas Street for cigarettes and more wine. The clerk, a fellow named Bob, recognized me. We had attended Patrick Henry High School together, where we had both been quietly acknowledged nobodies, not even on the debate or chess teams, or in the Glee Club, whatever the Glee Club did. Bonnie was a little drunk, but she knew how to excite a man. She twined her arm into mine and made a husky-voiced, bright-eyed show, writhing and crooning and giggling and showing off her teeth and neck.

Bob watched, mesmerized.

'Can I use your bathroom?' she said.

Bob almost broke his legs showing her where the restroom was in back. I surveyed the candy bars and studied my pimply face in one of the curved corner mirrors. I saw Bob coming up behind me, a pin-headed blob in the mirror. 'Where did you find her?' he said.

'We work together.'

'And you're what, out on a *date*?'

'Just drinking wine at her house.'

'Alone?'

'Yeah.'

'How did you do *that*? A fox like *that*. With bombs like *that*.' He bit his hand. His lips were all shiny and flecked with saliva.

'Take it easy, Bob. Do you want me to call a veterinarian?'

'Jesus,' he said. 'I couldn't get a date with my own sister. How did you do that?'

I shrugged. Now I knew what it was like to have a beautiful girl. It was not as Bob or I had imagined it. How did anything happen to you? It just happened.

'How old is she?' he demanded.

'Twenty-two.'

'She's old enough to buy *booze*.' He grimaced as if recalling spleen surgery. 'Oh, man, I'd kill for something like that. Has she got any friends?'

'I don't know.'

'How long have you been going out with her?'

'Just one night.'

'One night?' Bob spun around giddily, slapping his hip.

'Shhh,' I said. 'Here she comes.'

'What are you fellas whispering about?' she reprimanded hoarsely, wiggling her shoulders so the necklace on the top of her breasts jingled and slid. 'You're not talking about me, are you?'

We bought apple wine and Trues and waved goodbye. Bob stood alone in his bright little station and watched with melancholy wonder as we walked away.

'Look what I stole,' she said, when we were back in the car.

I looked down at a bubble package with a little tube of Blistex inside. 'What did you do that for?'

'It was right out there in the open. Nobody will miss it. You're not unhappy with me?'

'No, that's all right,' I said. 'Do you need it? I mean, do you use it?'

'No,' she said.

At three o'clock that morning we were sitting on the floor next to the stereo and it was time to make my move or fall asleep on the carpet like a good little Cub Scout. I had no knowledge of the passwords to carnality, but I had seen a lot of pornography in the hot lunch shops downtown. Annie Green Springs had filled me with sloppy confidence. And she was leaning back before me in steamy invitation, the buttons of her blouse coming undone, so I tossed off the last of my soda-pop wine and reached across to help her with the rest.

'What are you *doing*?!' she cried in a gruff tone that was meant to sound like reproof, but was instead almost trilling with delight.

'I am unbuttoning your blouse.'

'Are your intentions honorable?'

'My intentions are to take off your blouse.'

'Have you ever been with a woman before, Baby?'

'No,' I said.

'Are you sure you want this?'

'Why wouldn't I?'

'You might not.'

The word *transvestite* went off in my head, all those stories I had heard about the small-town (usually Navy) boy who meets the big-city girl and later on that night, to his horror, reaches down and honks the frankfurter. But she wasn't a transvestite. I wasn't that green. Then I thought *transsexual* (the husky voice, the pale masculine mouth, the weird fuzzy black eyes) — well, if he was a she, or however it worked, I thought, hats off to the surgeon! It was too late to turn back now.

'Not here, Baby,' she said, and led me by the hand down the hall. Her bed seemed to glow like an orange grove or a field of lilacs in the dusk. I was vertiginous with brimming, neck-cricking, hydrophobic ecstasy. I groped and grabbed like a blind suckling pig. Her body was sleek and splendid, abundant, refuting all notions of Scandinavian surgery. My jeans, in my robust haste, got jammed like a pair of handcuffs around my ankles. She asked me breathlessly, 'Are my titties too big?'

'God, no.'

'Is my pussy too tight?'

'No.'

'Some men think it's too tight.'

'No, it's just fine. It's perfect, honest, really...'

'You're very nice, Baby. You know that? I like nice men.'

She claimed to have five orgasms that night. I was lucky to have one. I humped and hunched away, like an insect with its head cut off. I seemed to be numb below the waist. My greatest fear had come true. I was not normal. I had masturbated too often, or dulled my senses by seeing too much sailor porno downtown.

For breakfast we ate Hostess Ho Ho's and Oscar Mayer smoked links on paper plates with plastic knives and forks. I had been sneaking glances in the mirror and congratulating myself whenever possible all morning. She sawed away at her smoked wienie. 'Baby,' she said. 'Would you consider moving in with me?'

'Moving in with you?'

'It's not too soon, is it?'

'Well, I hadn't —'

'I like you, Baby. I don't want to be alone...'

When I returned to my smelly, teenage apartment on Central Avenue that afternoon, Goldie and Woodchuck were sitting stoned at the kitchen table with Steve Jebets, one of the few people in the world I disliked. Jebets was a dark, square, blank-eyed lad with one permanent Alfalfa cowlick projecting from his side-parted hair. He drove a purple Buick Elektra 225 that his father had bought him and dressed as if he'd just escaped from a Saudi Arabian discotheque. He also worked for his father, a developer from the largest city in Pennsylvania, which Jebets pronounced 'Philadelthia.' Jebets made fun of my job as a hospital orderly. He said it was 'wiping assholes,' and that all orderlies were fags. Woodchuck, with the fine discriminating eye of a rhinoceros, had brought Steve Jebets into our ragged high-school group from his homeroom or somewhere. At nineteen, Jebets was thirty pounds bigger than me. One day I was going to take karate or work out with weights, and sock him in his Philadelthia kisser.

Smoke trailed up lazily from the mouth of a bong. Six raw and drug-drenched eyes stared at me. 'Where you been, man?' said Woodchuck, a burly, bucktoothed blond whose

hair still had a greenish tint from so many years on the high
school swim and water polo teams.

I could smell refried beans. J. Geils's *Full House* finished
and the needle arm swung back and parked itself in its cradle.
'Met a girl,' I said.

'What!?' Steve Jebets roared. '*You*?'

I moved straight to my bedroom and began to fill a
Chiquita banana box with clothes and shoes, my alarm
clock, and playing cards. Bonnie was waiting downstairs,
and I did not want her to change her mind and drive away
without me. I didn't want anything to do with Jebets either,
who liked to talk about all the women he'd had back in
Philadelthia. One time the summer before, he had seen me
with my sexy fifteen-year-old next-door neighbor, assumed
somehow she was my girlfriend, and tried to steal her from
me. Her real boyfriend, a welder, cut all four of his tires.

My buddies were all up now, standing in my bedroom
doorway, peering at me with their bloody gorilla eyes. 'What
are you doing?'

'I'm moving out.'

'Where?'

'With her.'

'You're fulla shit.' Jebets had brought with him from the
East a charming manner of speech, which included this
classic phrase and many other such unforgettable colloquial
gems as: 'ya shitbird,' 'them's are fightin' words,' and 'I'm
gonna play you the Nose Cracker Suite.' He whipped out
his comb and began to groom himself.

'Believe what you like,' I replied.

'Who is she?' he demanded.

'She's a carnival freak.'

'She must be,' said Jebets, touching up his perennial cowlick. 'What's her name?'

'Bonnie. She's an actress.'

'How old is she?'

'Twenty-two.'

'How many arms has she got?'

'Twenty-two.'

'That's less than three octopuses,' said Goldie, who was the only one in the room I liked at this moment because he was the only one who would not try to steal her from me.

'Octo-PIE,' I corrected.

'Octo-*pussies*,' crowed Woodchuck.

'She must be a pig,' said Jebets, returning the comb to his back pocket.

'No, pigs have four legs. Don't you remember? Now, if you'll excuse me,' I said, moving by them with my box. 'I'll make sure to drop you a card.'

'Hey, we'll come over,' Woodchuck shouted after me.

Not if I don't give you the address, I thought.

ON OUR FIRST NIGHT OFFICIALLY LIVING TOGETHER, BONNIE and I sat on the couch drinking wine and smoking Trues, and I kept telling myself, *I am living with a beautiful woman.* How had it happened? It was a miracle. It was like washing up on a desert island or stumbling into the lost regions of a remote African village. The carpet was like the smell of a thatch hut, and the wine was a special green hallucinogenic, and the plastic-filtered cigarettes were made from the poison put on arrows to shoot rare jungle birds from tree-tops. I felt like the top of my head had been planed off. That serene Neil Diamond girl with the sun hat looking down upon us from the wall seemed to be saying out the side of her mouth in a voice that sounded very much like Bob, the 7-11 clerk, 'You're living with a beautiful woman, ding-a-ling. How did you manage that?'

I watched Bonnie closely for the first two weeks because she was my girl and I was interested to know what in heaven's name she saw in me. Naturally, I knew something had to be wrong with her. I was willing to overlook a bit of alcoholism, that alarming donkey laugh, and what immediately became recognizable as kleptomania. I had to adjust to a nearly exclusive diet of cake from the grocery store and Oscar Mayer smoked links. Her ability to invent stories about herself bordered on the prodigious, but her memory was poor, so that she was constantly manufacturing new stories, which would clash with the perfectly good old ones. Her autograph of Keenan Wynn that I never saw, for example, turned into a collection of autographs of famous movie stars that I never saw. In the course of one day, her beloved only brother, who supposedly lived in Santa Monica, aged four years. Though she had lived there, she could not tell me where Topanga Canyon was, and one day as we stood in front of a franchise map of the U.S. at the International

House of Pancakes on El Cajon Boulevard and she tried
to show me where her modeling career had begun in a
Minnesota nunnery, she pointed to the upper peninsula of
Michigan. I had already been to the downtown library to
check a movie directory, cross-referencing Jason Robards,
Keenan Wynn, and *Double Damnation*, and found out that
such a film did not exist. But, as I say, I was willing to put
up with a few foibles, perhaps even a dangerous girl, because
I would not have had a girl otherwise.

Bonnie claimed, with a giggle, to be a nymphomaniac.
This may have been the one profession about herself, that
and her choice of cigarettes, that was true. I had no shortage
of sexual energy and undertook the task of satisfying her,
sometimes as many as five times a day, improving my skills
and potential for conjugal pleasure by lowering my expectations and occasionally conjuring up a smutty image from
one of the sticky-floored rooms downtown. Every night she
had dozens of orgasms, bushels of them, more than humanly
possible. Though it was the era of the orgasm, and there were
bestselling books about orgasms, and wise people from the
East commanded handsome lecture fees to discuss orgasms,
I learned to have a low opinion of them. In the currency of
orgasms there were too many counterfeits. And whatever
shudders of genuine bliss you might achieve, you never got
to keep one. You couldn't even remember them.

Every morning Bonnie scribbled, naked at the kitchen table,
in purple ink in a pink plush-bound diary that she locked
extravagantly with a tiny key inserted into a gold latch and 'hid'

in her underwear drawer. She liked to write naked in front of
me in the sunlight, her painted yellow hair tumbling across her
face and down her back, her foot up under her buttocks. As she
wrote she would glance at me frequently with mysterious smiles,
and say things such as: 'I bet you'd like to read this.'

I always told her I wouldn't, but I was actually very
curious. I would have liked to have known what she really
thought and felt. Unlike anyone I had spent considerable time
with, there was not one substantial thing I could claim to know
about her, except that she made Pinocchio look like Pope Paul
VI. And the truth about her was in that diary, I imagined. And
the truth about me was in there too.

BONNIE WAS SUPPOSEDLY AN ACTRESS LOOKING FOR WORK, BUT
the phone never rang. No one ever came to the door either,
except your general-issue Jehovah's Witness, and then one night
a ghetto kid with a box of chocolate bars, and then one other
time a neighbor wanting to know if we'd lost a cat. I assumed
that Bonnie had no friends — there was good reason to believe
this — but one night about nine o'clock, my night off, Bonnie
was burning sliced-off-the-tube chocolate chip cookies in the
kitchen, and I was sitting on the couch drinking apple wine and
watching a program about the manufacture of cheese on PBS
with the sound off and *Led Zeppelin One* playing on the turntable, when someone knocked on the door.

Bonnie dashed around the corner. 'Oh, Lance,' she cried,
falling out the door, her arms swinging around his neck like
ribbons around a maypole. 'Come in! Come in!'

I stood up, and my pants gathered into my crotch. Lance looked about twenty-three or twenty-four. He wore a striped harlequin sport shirt tucked into knife-pleat slacks and shiny, tan shoes that zipped up the sides. He seemed very confident to me and good looking in a languid, careless way, locks of his thick curly hair falling over his forehead.

Bonnie frolicked around the room in her long translucent floral evening gown, her breasts jiggling; she kept standing up on her toes and bringing her hands together against her throat. 'Come in. Come in. Sit down. Lance, oh, Lance, this is —' she seemed to forget my name for a moment — 'Baby.'

He smiled at me in the way you would smile at any adult named Baby. I shook hands with him and felt about as low and masculine as a snail. The arm on the turntable lifted from the record and we were left with a silent PBS cheese documentary. 'Nice to meet you,' he said.

Bonnie seemed out of breath. 'Can I get you a glass of wine, Lance?'

Lance sat down in the needlepoint rocking chair across from the couch. He must've made some affirmative sign on the wine offer, because Bonnie flew off into the kitchen. I studied Lance. He had an actor's good looks, except for a bulge in the middle of his top lip that pulled it back from the front teeth, and his eyes were a shade too far apart under the buttery locks of hair that fell over his forehead. It gave him the slightest appearance of imbecility. Also, the distance between his nose and mouth seemed a little long, especially with that knot on his lip.

Bonnie returned with a glass of wine. The brightly colored see-through gown made her look fat. I wanted her to look her best for company. I had only been able to show her off once, to Bob, a poor slob I barely knew, and only for a few minutes before she had stolen that tube of Blistex. I had been getting up the nerve to take her to a party and show her to the boys, though I knew my good friends would assume that anyone loose and crazy enough to fall for me would be fair game for them as well.

Lance accepted the wine, swung the ankle of his shiny, tan, zippered shoe up on a knee, and tipped back in the rocking chair. He took a sip from the wine, nodded contemplatively, then said to me, 'So, you're the one Bonnie has gone wild over, huh?'

'Well...' I blushed.

'Every time I talk to her that's all she can talk about, Baby, Baby, Baby...'

How often do you talk to her? I wondered, a flame of panic roaring up my spine.

Bonnie stood by with her own glass of wine and stared at Lance contentedly. She had neglected to ask if I wanted one. I could see her naked outline through the gown as she began to rub the back of Lance's neck.

I hastily lit a True, a funny name for a cigarette so technologically altered as to be difficult to identify as tobacco.

'Lance is an old acting friend of mine,' Bonnie explained, kneading Lance's neck without taking her eyes from him.

'Really?' I said, getting two or three puffs off the plastic-tipped cigarette, then flicking some ashes on my pants.

'Yes, we were in Strasberg together.'

'Is that in Germany?'

'No, that's an acting school.'

'Oh.' I grinned and took consecutive puffs off the True.

'We took lessons from Stella Adler.'

'Stella Adler.'

Lance nodded slowly. Bonnie had quit rubbing his neck. Now her hand lay on his shoulder. He seemed unaffected by the attention. His eyes had a soft, staring-into-the-fireplace look — a tender reminiscence of those Stella Adler days in Strasberg, Germany.

'She's Stanislavsky,' said Bonnie, to help me better understand the renowned Stella Adler.

'That's in Russia, right?'

The actors both laughed warmly. I was redeemed. Everything was going to be OK now.

'Lance is a method actor...like Al Pacino.'

'Ohhh.'

'He just did a margarine commercial.'

'Did he?'

'Yes. Blue Bonnet. Two hundred thirty-five people tried out for the part.'

'Think about that.'

'We acted together in San Francisco, when I lived there.'

'I didn't know you lived in San Francisco.'

'I never told you?'

I felt suddenly shaky, like a guy in a tree house who hears a loud crack. I had a sip of wine and lit up another cigarette. There was one still burning in the ashtray.

Lance smiled and patted Bonnie on the behind, calm and comfy as could be, ankle on knee. 'I need another glass of wine,' I announced. 'Anybody else need one?'

'What?'

I limped into the kitchen. The charcoal chip cookies were smoldering on the counter. I turned off the oven and dragged out the bottle of Annie Green Springs. As I poured the wine, I watched the bubbles gambol and wiggle to the top of my glass. The bottle was gone now. Bonnie would have to buy more. A sensible plan presented itself: I would go back into the room and say, 'Hey Bonnie, looks like we better run to the store for more wine. You want to come along with us, Lance? We can drop you off back where you came from, or the Mexican border, if you prefer...'

Bonnie was sitting in Lance's lap when I returned to the living room, her arm around his neck. 'Lance and I go way back,' she said to Lance.

I collapsed into the couch. Deranged voices came to me out of the fog. *Kill them with a kitchen knife*, they said. Bonnie kissed Lance on the neck and then looked over to check my reaction. When Lance slipped his hand inside her brightly colored gown, she looked at me again. Then she began to unbutton his shirt, continuing to monitor my responses as if she were tuning a car diagnostically. I felt myself petrifying. Her eyes were glittering zeroes, like a woman without a soul, like a woman in a Led Zeppelin song, and the bottom of her face had receded into mist, but the expression was: Aren't I a Naughty Girl? And shouldn't you just be outraged at me? Shouldn't you just kill us both in our tracks and put us into immemorial television history, either a trial or a mini-series? Aren't I the most wicked creature on earth, but aren't I having *fun*?

Lance didn't seem really to care one way or another how wicked or naughty she was or how high the flames around my face rose. He seemed to be enjoying her breasts.

The actors kissed in a sudden raging, foaming, violent, head-swaying, eyes-closed, nostril-huffing lock for a few minutes, Bonnie curled up and unbuttoned on his lap. Finally she stumbled up starry-eyed and took his hand, giving me a sweet, almost apologetic, but at the same time grim and dutiful, smile. Her face was a weird and fantastic convergence of sympathy, cruelty, and lust. It was like looking at a jigsaw puzzle that maniacs had hammered and glued together randomly. Lance's hair was a bit thrown out of place, his trousers were wrinkled and his shirt was unbuttoned, but other than that he seemed unruffled, the same cool, striding, almost robotic Lance that had walked through the door a half an hour before.

They left the bedroom door open for me. I was numb with disbelief. I had thought it impossible they would go this far. I knew that I should leave right then—but my car keys were in the bedroom. Also I wanted to give her a chance to explain herself. Maybe it was all some awful misunderstanding, or incredible arrangement of incompatible events. Temporary insanity. Hypnotism. An elaborate practical joke. A test of my fidelity. Maybe she was on medication.

And I did not know what the rules were. I had never even been out on a date. Everything I knew about women came from sailor porno, magazine articles, and late evening hearsay. Maybe if you were a skinny drip you had to share your women with thick-witted, Mediterranean-looking method actors.

I wandered into the kitchen and found a bottle of Ronrico rum below the sink next to the Clorox. I'd never had rum before. It tasted like rubbing alcohol. I took off my shoes and sat in the couch and gulped the Ronrico Rubbing Alcohol Rum as the greedy flames of humiliation crackled over the tops of my desiccated eyes. PBS had gone off the air. I listened to the bedsprings squeak and the headboard bang against the wall. Bonnie called out her pleasure in a series of hoarse and escalating moans.

I was still lying red-eyed and barefoot on the couch when the lovers emerged from the bedroom the next morning.

'You're still here?' said Bonnie wondrously.

'Where did you think I'd be?' I croaked.

Lance nodded and ran his fingers through his curly hair and yawned like the big lion after eating a whole zebra on a hot afternoon in the shade of a bimbo tree in Zimbabwe. The two lovers kissed sloppily at the door. Her hand lingered on his chest. He seemed irritated by her. She stood on her toes and breathed something light and hopeful in his ear. He mumbled and stumbled blankly out into the fiery, bright yellow sunlight.

Bonnie closed the door and clasped her hands behind her back. She looked wild and fearful and joyous all at the same time. Her hands fluttered to her lips. 'I thought you would—' she moved toward me. She wore a dippy tight-smiled, quick-eyed, and helpful expression, a Helpful-Mom-With-A-Long-Brain-Surgery-Scar expression. Her hands flipped on her wrists like trouts ashore.

'Oh, Baby, what do you think of me now?' she said. 'You must think I'm terrible.'

I moved past her to the bedroom to get my keys and pack my things. My foot was asleep, and I had a piercing pain in my left temple.

Bonnie followed me around the bedroom, jibbering. 'It was just a one-night thing,' she said. 'I don't know what happened.'

'That's fine,' I said.

'You're not leaving?'

'Of course I'm leaving.'

Bonnie gnawed the middle of a forefinger. 'Are you coming back?'

'Not unless I die or something,' I said, ripping one of my shirts off its hanger. 'Then I'll come back to HAUNT you.'

'Oh, Baby, Baby, I'm so sorry. I've hurt you.'

'Get out of my way. And stop calling me Baby. I'm not a Baby.' I grabbed my car keys and headed for the door.

'I bought you a gift,' she called. 'I was keeping it a surprise. I have it in the bedroom.'

I had to turn. 'Is everything you say a lie?'

'No, of course not.'

'You were never in a convent,' I said. 'You're not an actress. You don't know where Minnesota is. You don't have a gift for me.'

'I was too in a convent,' she retorted. 'We had ham and scalloped potatoes every Saturday night. And we had someone to love us who would never betray us.'

'Who?'

'Jesus, you stupid ass.'

I yanked open the front door. The sunlight was cold and startlingly bright and made my eyes ache. But it was something real anyway. The room behind me was not. The girl in it was not. I shut the door on the room and the girl that were not real, and all the ham and scalloped potatoes, and plodded numbly down the stairs. It was chilly out, the air copper-thin; nothing to filter the sunlight except for the smell of geraniums and a vapor of eucalyptus dust. I heard the door open behind me. She came to the rail and looked down at me imploringly, bosoms spilling, arms spread, her big, dark eyes like holes in the universe. 'I didn't mean to call you a stupid ass. I don't want to be alone. I don't love Lance anymore. Give me another chance,' she said. 'I promise I'll never do it again. Please.'

I stopped, which was a mistake, and felt sorry for her, which was a mistake, and believed her, which was another mistake, but as she had said, I was a nice guy. And the part about Jesus got me, even if she was making it up. And I had nowhere to go except back to Woodchuck and Goldie's place to explain to their leering faces how I had lost my girl. And my dress shoes were still in her closet. And my alarm clock was on her bed stand. And a family-pack of breaded veal cutlets I had bought at the store only a day before lay yet unopened in her freezer.

I decided to give her another chance.

A WEEK LATER GOLDIE, WOODCHUCK, AND JEBETS FINALLY showed up at my door. I'd been waiting for them. 'How did you find me?' I said, like the weary fugitive holding out his wrists to the FBI.

'We went to the hospital,' said Jebets. 'The dyke nurse told us.'

When Bonnie came around the corner, she sprang to life. 'Good afternoon, gentlemen,' she said. 'Come in. Sit down. You didn't tell me you had friends, Baby. And such handsome boys.'

They shuffled in self-consciously, their simpering expressions still articulating doubt about my ability to live with a woman, even a kidnapped geriatric held hostage in a wheelchair. I was the youngest of my group, the least physically mature, the least aggressive, the least athletic. I was the mascot. I was supposed to watch them succeed and clap exuberantly on the sidelines. I could tell they wanted to knock all the air out of my stomach with their elbows.

'Sit down anywhere,' I said.

Woodchuck and Goldie tumbled into the couch. Jebets folded himself into a sitting position, Japanese-style, before the coffee table.

I made introductions. Bonnie beamed. 'Would you fellas like some wine?'

'Sure,' they all chimed. 'I brought some dope,' added Goldie. 'It's Hawaiian.'

'Light it up, Sparky,' said Bonnie.

It was good pot and soon we were rendered useless. Bonnie flitted about the room, changing records, filling wine glasses, and dropping over at the waist to share her breasts like a tray of hors d'œuvres. 'You boys hungry?' she said.

'Yeah, well OK.' They grinned at one another. What a party. With a girl and everything.

Smoked links were served.

'This is my kind of munchie,' Jebets announced, reminding me of the night the previous summer when he tossed off a pint of Four Roses whiskey in twenty-three seconds. (*Just add alcohol*, goes the saying). About twenty-three seconds later he was blowing long puddles of beans and wienies all over the kitchen floor, the miniature frankfurters perfectly intact.

'I'm a big wienie eater myself,' Bonnie agreed. 'By that I mean to say I eat a lot of wienies. Not necessarily big wienies.' She smiled and squinted with her front teeth stuck out. 'Though I like big wienies.'

My good friends laughed and gave me nervous side glances. Jebets, a devoted and outspoken breast man, stared unabashedly with the frustrated knit brow of the hound as Bonnie moved about the room. Eventually she was sitting on the floor next to him, their knees touching. She flirted with about as much subtlety as a Fifth Street prostitute.

When she checked over at me with that Aren't I a Naughty Girl expression, I felt the tape of Lance began to replay. Slow-motion ruin. Dyspepsia. I lurched up, my face burning, and limped into the kitchen for more wine. On the counter a swarm of ants was plundering a clot of ketchup.

I heard Bonnie saying: 'I had a small part in a movie with Eliot Gould. I have his autograph.'

'Really,' said Jebets. 'Can I see it?'

'It's at my mother's house.'

'Where does your mother live? Maybe we could go over there.'

'Hey, do you want to go the store? We need some more wine.'

'I'm not old enough.'

'I am.'

'I'll go,' shouted Woodchuck.

Bonnie grabbed Jebet's hand. 'No, sit down, Beaver. We're gonna take my car. There's only enough room for two.' She winked at me. 'We'll be back in a jiff.'

The door opened, blinding me with that patented Landis Street Heartbreaker Sunlight. Then they were gone.

Woodchuck and Goldie sat on the couch staring at me sympathetically. An hour passed. 'Well, we'd better go,' they said at last.

'You need a ride?'

'No, we got Goldie's van.'

I saw my friends to the door. I watched Goldie's orange Chevy van turn left out of the parking lot. Then I went into Bonnie's bedroom, found her diary, broke the lock, and began to read. The handwriting was messy and purple with big juvenile loops and pitiful spelling. I sat on the bed and turned the pages. The name 'Lance' appeared several hundred times, but my own was not mentioned once. There was not even an indirect reference to anyone who resembled me. I was not much, but to live with a woman twenty-four hours a day for more than a month and give her thousands of orgasms and not be mentioned once in her diary was unfathomable to me. She could've at least written: 'I am living with a geek, I can't remember his name, so I call him Baby,' but I was more anonymous than that. It was staggering to be such a nonentity. It was like being thrown down a time tunnel back into high school. I slammed the book shut and returned it broken-locked to its drawer. Then I repacked my Chiquita banana box, not forgetting my dress shoes and alarm clock this time, and drove down to the beach to spend a week or two with my best friend Dewy Daldorph, the devout Christian, who regardless of his phase — junior mafioso or tropical island smuggler — always treated me as if I were his brother.

Bonnie did not show up at Pine Manor the next day. I was braced for the embarrassment, the possible scene, but she never worked, as far as I know, in a hospital again. The head nurse, who had seemed appalled by my alliance with Bonnie Newton, appeared relieved to see her gone and said in effect, 'Good riddance.' A few days later Goldie and Woodchuck came into the hospital and found me in Mr. Hollins's room, tying him up in his wheelchair by the window. My visiting buddies usually wore humble and horrified expressions on their red-eyed faces as they negotiated the hospital aisles, as if old age and decrepitude could only happen to you by accidental contact. Today, however, they were buoyed and immunized by the titillation of my delightfully bad fortune.

'Did you hear the news, man?'

'No.'

Their eyes explored my face thoroughly. 'Bonnie and Jebets are getting married.'

I laughed. I remember thinking how wonderful the sun was shining through the water spots on the window, how exquisite it was to be free.

I think they thought I was hurt and putting on an act.

IN THE MIDSUMMER OF 1973, MISSION BEACH WAS A NARROW, four-mile-long strip of hodgepodge cottages between the Pacific Ocean and Mission Bay. The foggy, rusting little beach community contained two small grocery stores, two liquor stores, a rental shop, a rickety old amusement park, a long, busy cement boardwalk with a three-foot seawall, an Italian sub shop called Toby's, a couple of bars that changed hands every few months, and the usual lonesome hot-dog stand.

Dewy lived on the bayside on Redondo Court in a tiny, rough, brown bungalow filled with bamboo furniture and unread *Time* magazines. The interior walls were a smooth gray Edvard Munchian driftwood theme. Off to the right was a kitchen so small you had to use a short-handled spatula to turn your eggs. The seaweed-colored shag carpet offered up the aroma of wet dog, beach, and Dewy's particularly pungent feet. Dewy had sold the dog. He should've sold his feet. I would've liked to have had the dog. The place was still infested with fleas. They leaped like little pogo-stick artists, PWINK! PWINK! across the floor.

I ended up staying with Dewy for more than a year. We rarely saw each other. He worked days, I worked nights. He was gone much of the time, visiting his girl, doing church projects, or absorbing fatherly advice from Al, his craps-and-racetrack-loving mafioso boss at Caruso's, the downtown restaurant where he was the day manager. Tall and bearded with an athlete's build, Dewy looked twenty-five, but he was eighteen going on fifteen, the age at which his family had fallen apart, father sayonara, mother gone to sauce. My parents had rescued him. He lived with us until he finished high school. Dewy wanted the world to know he was grown up so he showed it manly things: hard work, big new trucks, Chinese food to go, not paying his parking tickets, and handguns. On my second night staying with him, he proudly produced his new .357 magnum, a chrome, walnut, and iron contraption he kept wrapped in tissue paper in a box under his bed. 'It's a beauty, isn't it?'

'Yeah, gorgeous.'

'It'll blow a door off its hinges,' he muttered reverently. 'And take a guy's leg clean off. He'll bleed to death before the ambulance gets there.'

'Gracious sakes,' I said.

He shoved it at me. 'Here, take it.'

'No, really.'

'Take it. I want you to have it.'

I accepted it awkwardly, turning it over in my hands. It was as cold and heavy as a corpse. I disliked guns. I handed it back. 'Put it away.'

'Look,' he said, breaking the chamber open. He emptied the rounds, then inserted them again. 'See? It's just a tool. Evolution, man. You've got to adapt. You take this one. I've already got a .38 in the car.'

'What would I do with it?'

'Carry it, man. Guy up on the boardwalk got robbed two days ago.'

'Thanks anyway.'

'I mean, if somebody breaks in or something or tries to rob you, what are you going to do?'

'Blow their leg off and watch them bleed to death before the ambulance gets there?'

'You don't need to shoot anyone,' he said. 'Just show it.'

'Right,' I said, 'and then shoot myself in the foot.'

'OK,' he said, putting it away with a sigh. 'It's there if you change your mind. Just remember to put it back in the box when you're done with it...'

For many days, like a good little Pandora, I left that box alone, but one night, out of idleness and a *Hawaii Five-O* rerun I'd already seen seven times, I dragged the six-shooter out. It was beautiful, in a way, gleaming and obscene, a lamp unto fear. I turned it over in my hands, my index fingers enclosing the trigger like a baby's legs reflexively encircling its mother's waist. It took me a while to figure out how to break open the chamber. I slid the bullets in and out. The barrel was short, about four inches' worth. I held the weapon along my hip and whipped it straight up and made some convincing gunshot sounds with my mouth. I sighted a picture on the wall. Then I sighted the lamp, pretending it was Jebets, which gave me more satisfaction than I expected. That night I carried the gun with me down the beach. I was as swollen as a tick with power. I was as intoxicated as a man with two penises. I waited for some guys just out of prison to fool with me. The world was surprisingly peaceful. But then some frustrated young man in a trench coat was shouting at his girlfriend up by the seawall, and I actually thought about walking up there and pointing the gun at him to straighten him out. That's when I realized how easy it would be to kill someone for no good reason, and I went home and put the revolver back in its box under the bed where it belonged.

I WAS EMBARRASSED ABOUT HAVING MY ONE AND ONLY GIRL stolen out from under me, so I began taking out other nurse's aides. Getting women, especially nurse's aides, who were often lonely and outnumbered me twelve to one, was suddenly easy. I had inadvertently, with the long practice high school had given me, discovered the essential trick in capturing women's interest, which was to ignore them entirely. Living with Bonnie probably had something to do with my success too. These curious little creatures had seen me with Bonnie and that somehow stamped me normal or perhaps even dangerous. Sex, though it was not half of what had been promised to me by popular culture, had helped to cure my acne. I had some pretty girlfriends and some ugly ones too. The ugly ones were not always the best in bed, as the legend goes, and neither were they any more grateful. They were also harder to get rid of. I would always take the pretty ones down to the 7-11 in North Park to watch Bob writhe in jealous amazement.

In mid-December the first love letter arrived. My admirer was supposedly anonymous, but I recognized the leaky, purple, graceless hand. 'I can't live another day without you,' Bonnie wrote. 'I guess you would say that I am obcesed.' I read the letter again, nonplussed. I knew that she didn't love me. What could have possibly changed? A shred of curiosity remained, but it was overridden by a sense of unease. I didn't want to encourage her. And she was married now. I threw the letter away.

More letters followed. They had the same mushy, lost, and

disturbing tone as the Scrabble notes we had passed long ago on Landis Street. I stopped opening them after a while.

Then the phone rang one night. It was late February. Dewy was off with his Nazarene girlfriend. I answered on the first ring. 'It's me, Baby,' said the husky feminine voice.

'Who's me?' I said.

'I need to talk to you,' she said.

'How did you get my number?'

'Can we talk?'

'Go ahead and talk.'

'I mean, can we meet somewhere?'

'Why?'

'Because I need your help.'

'What kind of help?'

'I'm the one who's been writing the letters.'

'I know that.'

'Then you know you're the only one who can help me.'

I agreed to meet her. I could watch her now with scientific detachment, laugh and leave whenever I pleased. I had turned eighteen long ago, in November, and I felt wise with loss and age.

We met on the B Street Pier. I parked and climbed into her little soup can of a horsehair-smelling MGB so I could leave when I wanted without her getting tangly on me. She looked better than I remembered. She wore a red, low-cut sweater and a very short skirt and white knee stockings. I rolled down the window and lit a cigarette. The towering tuna boats were all nestled in for the night, bobbing and scraping gently against their rubber slips. One low, late-night barge scooted out along the light-rippled surface of the water. The air smelled hazily of creosote and diesel fuel.

'I don't have long,' I said. 'I've got some laundry I need to do.'

'I'm glad you came,' she said. 'I feel so awful.'

'About what?'

'About, you know—Lance and Steve and everything.'

'Don't,' I said, trying to stretch out my legs. 'I've forgotten it. It was all so stupid.'

'Wasn't it?'

'What did you want to talk to me about?'

'I've been seeing a psychiatrist,' she said, the flesh in the space between her eyes crimping suddenly. 'He told me I was obsessed with you.'

'Obsessed,' I said.

'I told him about everything, Lance and everything, the big mistake I made…and do you know what he says?'

'That you should be admitted to a psychiatric hospital?'

'No, he says I should sleep with you.'

'The psychiatrist said that?'

'Yes. He says that an obsession is in the mind and once it is played out in reality it can no longer be an obsession.'

I wanted to ask her what it would be when it was no longer in the mind, but her skirt was shrinking. She mussed her hair and rustled in her seat and turned to face me, the skirt climbing up her legs. 'Do you want to come talk to him?'

'Who? A psychiatrist?'

'Yes, he'd like you to come in. He wants to meet you.'
She laughed nervously in her coffee-grinder voice. 'I've
talked so much about you.'

'Me? No. I don't want to see a psychiatrist.'

She put her fingers lightly on my shoulder. 'My marriage isn't working, Baby. I made a mistake...'

I looked up the tall, green hull of a fishing boat called
the *Samurai Sunrise*. 'So what do you want me to do about
it?'

She swatted me and smiled, squinting her eyes dreamily.
'I want to sleep with you, Silly.'

'Sleep with me?' I said.

'I love you.'

'No, you don't, Bonnie. I read your diary.'

'You shouldn't have done that.'

'You shouldn't have lied to me.'

'I keep my lives separate,' she said. 'The diary was my
dirty life.'

'I don't believe you. Anyway, you're married.'

'Just once,' she said. 'I need it. He won't know. He's off
at a bar. He's seeing another woman. We're getting a divorce.
I need it, Baby. I need you...'

I took her back to Dewy's beach bungalow. I didn't care about
her one way or the other—but I wanted revenge on Jebets for
stealing her from me. And she looked good. Nature had built
Bonnie for rolling in the sheets, that was it, and there was no
sense wasting her. We stopped along the way and bought a bottle
of strawberry wine. The streets were puddled in fog. The fog

swept in from left to right in a cold steady flow. The streetlights glowed in lacy blobs like odd little suns in the mist.

We parked down by the Yacht Club, just past the old Santa Clara Hotel. The lot was nearly empty. A tiny, Asian-looking man was rummaging through a trashcan. Two hooded figures in black moved like phantoms down through the alley. Across the street the ocean riffled and roared with a babbling noise in the background like the laughter of nuns on a forbidden picnic.

'This is a nice little place,' she said, looking around and setting her purse on the bamboo couch. 'A beach hut. It's so romantic.'

A flea bounced spectacularly out of the carpet and receded again. 'It's not mine,' I said, pouring two glasses of the foamy, sweet Boone's Farm Strawberry wine. I noticed she was shivering and lit the little wall furnace, filling the cottage with the smell of burnt lint and gas.

'I've got to get back pretty soon,' she said. 'He'll be looking for me.'

I turned off all the lights, and we kissed for a while. Her mouth tasted like brussels sprouts, and she seemed slightly heavier around the hips. 'I want to do something for you,' she said, taking my wrist hungrily.

I followed her into the bedroom, flinging off my shirt and socks. Her skirt dropped to the floor. One of her crumpled stockings rocketed past my eyes. Our jaws met in a sliding, heated, teeth-clashing moan. I felt her hot flat thigh, and kissed her neck, and bit her tiny earrings.

'Put this pillow under me,' she said. 'Oh, yes.'

Now someone was knocking on the door.

'Forget it,' Bonnie moaned.

I kissed the cup of her throat, the crease of her arm. The knocking insisted, louder with each series. Then a few very pronounced thumps and a familiar voice that boomed: 'BONNIE! I know you're in there!'

Bonnie leaped back against the wall. I fell and banged my forehead on her knee.

'It's Steve,' she cried.

'Jebets,' I said, wild-eyed, rubbing my head.

'Let me in!' cried Jebets, with a few more slams on the door panel.

'How does he know you're here?'

'He must've followed us. He must have been looking in the window.' She cowered in the corner, the sheet drawn up over her breasts.

'Hey, I know you're in there,' bellowed Jebets, 'and if you don't let me in I'm going to break down the fucking door.'

'Don't let him in,' gasped Bonnie.

I scrambled up and snapped on the lights. Clothes were everywhere, draped over the dresser, hanging from door-knobs. A pink sock dangled from the lamp shade. Bonnie crouched in her corner, a frozen Chihuahua grin on her face. I pulled on a pair of pants.

'You did this on purpose,' I said.

'He'll kill us if you let him in,' she said.

A fist hit the door and the wood cracked. 'Bonnie, you stinking two-timing whore — let me in there...'

'Just a minute!' I shouted amiably, reaching under the bed and sliding out the shoe box. Bonnie's eyes bulged as the tissue paper fell away from the gleaming revolver. I made a quick expert check to see if it was loaded. It was.

Jebets drummed the door with his fist and pieces of wood began to fly.

'I'll kick it in,' he announced.

'It isn't my door,' I said.

'You little shitbird,' he said. 'I'm gonna tear you to pieces.'

'I've got a gun,' I warned, standing two feet from the door, 'and I'm poised to fire.'

Bonnie was behind me now, wrapped in a sheet. 'Shoot him, Baby,' she said.

A huge stick of varnished wood came spinning out at me as he struck again. 'Stop or I'll shoot,' I said. 'I swear to God, Jebets, I'll shoot.'

'Shoot him, Baby.'

He struck the door again and I was so desperate and afraid for my life that I squeezed the trigger, aiming high on the door, hoping only to scare him, and then I was twisted around to the right, adjusted for the recoil, and tried to figure out why the gun hadn't discharged. It was faulty equipment. No, I had forgotten to release the safety. Truth be known, I did not know what a safety was.

The door came toppling down. Bonnie screamed and ran for the bedroom, knocking over a glass of strawberry wine.

Jebets, scarlet with fury, a wood chip in his hair, lunged past me. 'Come back here, you dumb little bitch.'

'I'm not going with you!' she cried.

I stared at the gun and shook it a couple of times. Then I watched the spreading wine stain in the carpet.

'Get your clothes, slut!' he shouted at her. 'Where are your goddamn clothes?'

She began to sob.

I dropped the gun into the couch and found a cigarette.

'Let me get dressed,' she pleaded. 'Please.'

'Do you want a beer?' I said to Jebets.

He shot me a furious, exasperated, and yet somehow sheepish glare. It was the only time we would ever share a particle of sympathy for each other, all made possible by Bonnie and her genius for scenes. 'Yeah,' he said, his jaw muscles squirming like garter snakes.

'In the refrigerator,' I said. 'Help yourself.'

Jebets stomped into the kitchen, yanked open the little icebox, ripped the cap off a bottle, and took a couple of angry swigs.

Bonnie dawdled. Jebets finally hauled her out by the arm, dragging her across the broken threshold, the sheet still wrapped around her.

Not long after this, Bonnie and Steve would have a child. While she was pregnant she would drink, smoke, and take many drugs, including methamphetamine and LSD. The child would not only turn out to be healthy and normal, but intelligent and beautiful. Jebets would divorce Bonnie

after three years, develop a serious methamphetamine problem, chain smoke those awful Trues, spend all his free time
at the topless bars, and then one day, frightened by a sudden
starboard glimpse of that towering, dark archipelago called
Death, he would steer down hard and straighten his course,
quit the drugs, remarry a decent woman, and find some
time for his twelve-year-old child. But it would be too late.
He would die of a heart attack at the age of thirty-two.

Bonnie didn't last long either. She disappeared shortly after
the divorce, leaving her child behind. The last time I saw
her was late at night in Mission Beach. I was returning from
a long walk and she was standing by herself under a lamp
by the seawall at Rockaway Court. A white fur coat was
thrown around her neck and she wore beige Capri slacks that
bulged at the hips. She stared at me forlornly. It was winter-
time again. All along the boardwalk the cottages were dark. I
thought she would follow me or call to me as I walked wordlessly away, but when I turned back around I was all alone
under the stars.

Failure of a Man Named Love

IT WAS FRIDAY NIGHT, CLOSING TIME AT THE SHIMMY JOY, THE downtown Third Street, Niagara Falls, New York, singles nightclub where I worked as a bartender four nights a week. I was drunk as usual, telling myself one of these days pretty soon (before it was too late) it would be time to quit. The bouncers waded through the mob, bellowing threats, throwing stools up on tabletops. A few customers clung to the counter, pleading for one last drink. I glanced at the door, hoping Charlene would show.

It was the dead, deep winter of 1983. Niagara Falls was in bad shape, its people moving out, its lakes and river poisoned by manufacturing, unemployment around twenty-five percent. Much of the automobile industry, the lifeblood of Western New York, was crippled or shut down. Niagara Falls was the home of Love Canal, the environmental disaster of the decade, a housing development built on top of a chemical dump site, now fenced off and posted, the windows boarded up, a ghost town sinking amid dead trees in a quagmire of toxic waste.

With unemployment, the number of bars in Niagara Falls had doubled in the last two years. Many people had also turned to selling drugs to make a living. Cocaine was the drug of choice. Third Street even had its own pusher, a likeable mush-mouthed loser named Weasel, who made his nightly bar-to-bar rounds in a trench coat lined with glittering packets of 'product.' Weasel liked to wrap up his evenings at the Shimmy Joy, where the late crowds were best. Unless he had sold out, he usually enjoyed an entourage of devoted, tail-wiggling, shiny-lipped females. Tonight he arrived with three. In 1983 there was no need to waste your time reading *How to Pick Up Attractive Women*; all you needed for shallow virile success was gold neck jewelry and one or two packets of Weasel's Witless Whoopee Powder (guaranteed to cure shyness, rancor, and unpopularity for as long as twenty minutes). I glanced at the door, hoping Charlene would show. Weasel waved at me, mush-mouthed a greeting ('Yo, bro... [*unintelligible*]') and, though the bar was closed, I poured him a drink, Amaretto on the rocks.

I had come to Niagara Falls the year before to cook in the restaurant of a friend, who moved to Washington D.C. three weeks after his restaurant failed. I had just turned twenty-eight. Charlene, an engineer at Harrison Radiator in Buffalo, who'd been laid off and was now waiting tables, was twenty-four. She was not a very nice girl. I was no Mahatma Gandhi myself. When I first began to date Charlene, the people who knew her warned me. 'Won't work.' 'Wrong girl.' 'You'll be sorry.' But there were many things to like about her: her unpretentiousness, her aloofness, a certain reckless *sang-froid*. With diamond black eyes and long dark hair, she was lithe and brainy, small breasted and tall. She had read and admired *Jude the Obscure*. She had an engineering degree from SUNY Buffalo. A hearty Czechoslovakian girl, she could drink all night and was great in bed. Unfortunately she slept around. And to teach her a lesson, so did I. Though I was on the verge of straightening out my life, etc., Charlene seemed unaffected by her barren and dissolute existence. Each time she found out I had been with another woman, all she wanted to know was, 'Is she prettier than me?'

I counted my tips: fifty, a good night. Charlene didn't show. To hell with her, I thought. I convinced myself I would get rid of her soon, straighten out my life, etc., and drove to an after-hours place. I must've known two thousand people in NFNY. If I didn't know their names, I knew what they drank. Being a bartender at a popular nightclub is like being captain of the high school football team. Everyone knows your name. They wave and smile and want to be seen with you, want to buy you a drink. I hit three after-hours places (hoping, despite myself, to find Charlene) before I finally ran into Oz, who invited me over to his house on Grand Island.

Oz was a third-owner of the Shimmy Joy. Once he'd had a good-paying job with GM, now he had a better-paying position with the Colombian Drug Cartel. He wore a purple kimono and glided along like a phantom on wheels. He was a big-time coke dealer, but he'd broken the cardinal rule and gotten himself hooked on the product. He smoked cocaine. We called it freebasing. There was no word yet for crack. Oz cooked it up in the kitchen and brought it into the living room on an engraved stainless steel platter: big, amorphous, soapy yellow chunks. It was a secret art. He was the only one who knew how to do it — except I'd watched him from around the corner, and I knew how to do it too.

We gathered around the wet bar in the corner of the living room in the dark, leather-furnished, wood-smelling home with the television always on. Oz inspected his equipment: a large glass pipe with a globe-shaped chamber, a dozen dime-sized brass screens, a box of Q-tips, and a bottle of Bacardi 151. There were five of us, the so-called elect, including Kirsten, a comely college student, and Wondra, a sexy cocktail waitress, both regulars along the strip of bars on Third Street. Oz called the women who were attracted to his drugs 'cocaine harlots.' They didn't seem to mind. He was always good for a couple of grand. He lit a candle. His rings glittered. The sleeves of his kimono rustled like a surplice as he dipped a Q-tip into the rum.

The first inhaled hit of volatilized cocaine is the best: it launches you through the roof of the sky. There is no greater high. It makes an orgasm seem like a stubbed toe. You love, with the power of God, all things: house plants, bumblebees, lint balls, even the cat shit in the sandbox beneath the sink. I thought of Charlene and loved her for once purely, without resentment or remorse, without a trace of indignation for having neglected me. I longed to share this feeling with her, this unfathomable, infallible, and virtuous love. So I called her apartment but she wasn't home.

At 5 a.m. the other two owners of the Shimmy Joy arrived. The glass pipe, its walls caked with alkaloid snowflakes, its smoldering brass screens dripping with Babylonian dreams, floated from hand to hand, jolting and frying *medulla oblongatas* and greedily scorching one pair of already scorched and scarlet lungs after the next. We babbled in exhaustive refrains like overcaffeinated housewives at a high school reunion: '...you know, I've always wanted to tell you what a great person I think you are...' As the sun blossomed in the curtains the sense of fellowship began to drain. The conversation waned. I caught my waxy, inebriated image in the mirror. Oz yanked down the shades and glided into the kitchen to cook up some more.

I stumbled back to work at 5 p.m. like something dragged up from a lake: no sleep, not even time for a shower. I felt as if I'd traveled around the sun, like a bag of charcoal with legs. I had to get drunk to make it through. The customers broke in waves against the bar. I spilled drinks, dropped glasses, gave the wrong change. The owners didn't care. They were freebasing over at Oz's. About eleven o'clock, Charlene coasted imperially through the door and down through the crowd, nudging into the only open space at the end of the bar, the plastic buttons of the cigarette machine glowing red and green behind her. I was too wrecked to go down and say hello. I didn't feel like listening to her anyway. She flared her nostrils at me.

Eventually she made her way down to my end and leaned into me for a kiss. I took in her scent, peanuts and ashes and Cherry Sucrets. As long as I was incapacitated and uninterested in being with her, as long as I could put into doubt her ability to attract, she would remain at the bar.

'What's wrong with you?' she said.

I fixed her a drink, vodka and iced tea, with lemon. 'Where were you last night?' I said.

'Oh,' she answered aloofly. 'I went swimming.'

'Where?'

'At Gene's,' she said. Gene was a bartender, who lived in a complex with an indoor pool. 'There was a party there,' she said. 'What about you?'

'I went to Oz's.'

She set her hand on her hip. 'Why didn't you call me?'

'I did. Four thirty in the morning. You were probably in the pool, drunk in your bikini.'

She wrinkled her face as if she'd just swallowed the lemon wedge in her drink. 'Who all was there?'

'I have to get back to work,' I said, shoving away. 'I'll talk to you later.'

When the Shimmy Joy closed at two, I was embalmed, a flat EEG, not enough energy to pull on the cigarette dangling from my lips. Charlene lingered, closely monitoring all the women who smiled at or talked to me. I told her as she left that I would see her tomorrow, which meant that she would disappear for a week. If I really wanted to see her tomorrow I would've said, 'It's over between us, Charlene. I've started seeing someone else.'

I didn't see Charlene for nine days. But I called her up twice and listened to the telephone ring. I imagined her apartment, crossword puzzle books on the couch, doilies draped over the television, empty Diet Coke cans, the portrait of Mother Cabrini on the wall above the dining-room table. Two friends told me they had seen her several nights 'swimming' at Gene's. On Friday, after work, the one night I could usually count on her to show (at least for a few minutes to make sure I was still miserable), she was nowhere to be found. I found revenge in the form of a meaningless liaison named Gina Bonaventure, a Niagara University psychology major with a weakness for bartenders and whoopee powder.

The next night Charlene strolled into the Shimmy Joy late, drunk with her girlfriend, Pamela, who worked in a pharmacy. Pamela was broad shouldered with short bangs and big gums, and she dressed for her nights out barhopping as if she were stepping up to the podium to accept her Oscar for Best Actress. Charlene sidled up to the end of the bar. We kissed. I smelled Scotch in her hair.

'I'm toasted,' she said.

'Congratulations.'

'Don't be snotty.'

'Been so long since I've seen you I almost forgot what you looked like. What are you having?'

'Two vodka and teas.'

'I'll have a greyhound,' sniffed Pamela, regally raising her chin.

Charlene rummaged through her purse for a cigarette. 'I heard you went out with Gina.'

I filled glasses with ice. 'I heard you went swimming.'

She tossed her head. 'Once.'

Pamela scowled at me. Like many of Charlene's close drinking companions, Pamela disliked me.

Eager customers were beginning to lean over the bar through the gaps, holding up their empty glasses.

'I gotta go,' I said. 'You be home later?'

She lit a cigarette and snapped out the flame. 'I'll be home.'

Pamela slashed my image to pieces with her eyelashes. Charlene looked off into an imaginary distance. The two women left before they'd finished their drinks.

Later that night Charlene was not home. I waited in front of her house in my car for an hour, looking up at the dark icy windows. Finally I left. I saw her car approaching from the other direction, but I didn't bother to slow down or wave. I didn't want to admit that it was over between us, that I had failed (again), that all the people who warned me were right, that my ability to make judgments was unchanged, that I had started over only to repeat every mistake I had ever made, that my life was not a long unlucky streak but a carefully and even beautifully tragic self-made design, that I was like Wayne Newton—maybe a different hotel, but the same show night after night.

Charlene lived in the LaSalle District, only two miles from Love Canal. In 1892 an entrepreneur named William T. Love had tried to construct a canal between the Niagara River and Lake Ontario, but abandoned the project with the arrival of the economic depression of 1893. Eventually the land was sold to a chemical firm named Hooker, who filled the chasm with an estimated 21,000 tons of chemical waste. In 1953, with the old canal packed to the brim, Hooker covered it with dirt and sold it off to the local Board of Education for a buck, not neglecting to include a clause that relieved them from any future liability incurred by the waste. An elementary school was erected on the site and the remaining land was sold to developers. Houses went up and hundreds of families moved in. It wasn't long before 21,000 tons of noxious chemicals began bubbling up through the ground. Children burned their feet on the lawns, basements filled with strange gases. Miscarriage, birth defect, and cancer rates soared. The *60 Minutes* crew raced to the scene and tumbled salivating out of their vans. In August of 1978, the state of New York declared a medical State of Emergency. Five days later, Jimmy Carter declared the Love Canal area a federal emergency. Two hundred thirty-nine families were evacuated; the neighborhood was closed down and sealed off.

I drove down to Love Canal that night. I often strolled these abandoned grounds to think. I felt at home here. No one bothered me. The old toxic ghost town was more silent and peaceful than any graveyard. There wasn't the faintest

sign of life, not a bug or a flower or a bird. My tracks through
the virgin green moonlit snow marked the only traces of a
living human soul. The mists crept low around the corners
of the houses and the cold air reeked faintly of sauerkraut
and chloroform. Before the poisons were discovered and the
people moved out, this was a neighborhood much like the
one I'd grown up in, with its trim little houses, square little
lawns. Swing sets. Clotheslines. I passed a sign that said DEAF
CHILD AREA. I saw a tricycle covered with snow in a driveway.
The wind moaned and the cloud-veiled moon shone down
through the dead, ice-crusted trees. I listened — children
screaming, barbecues blazing, dogs barking, the squeak of
swings, laundry rumpling in the breeze. Ghost sounds.

On the way back to the car I decided to leave, to really
leave, not only my hopelessly abysmal and dissolving horror-
house sweetheart and my poisoned Honeymoon City, but
my own stagnant drunken empty life. I wondered what
Charlene would do when I told her I was leaving. I pictured
her dabbing her eyes in mock sorrow, then yawning. I didn't
think it was possible that she would understand I really meant
it this time.

Four days, two motels, and sixteen cups of coffee later, I
was sitting in a Tarzana Denny's with my mom and dad at a
little table in the center of the room, eggs down below me,
the plump yolks shimmering in a pool of grease, and my
mother saying: 'We're glad to have you back.'

My father, his face a jug of red wine, his dark coiled Greek
black hair invaded with gray, beamed at me. He had just

come up from San Diego. My mother had recently left him. My father was Wreck Number One, drunk every night, though he had quit drinking for weeks now to try and win her back.

'Do you have any plans?' my mother said.

The sun poured down through the windows. I took a drink of my orange juice. 'I don't have any plans.'

'Are you going to stay around for a while?'

I picked up my fork and pierced one of the yolks. Two waitresses in tight brown polyester with full trays almost collided. A whole crowd of what looked like church people filed in through the door, and there was nowhere for them to sit. 'I don't know,' I said.

'Why don't you eat?'

'He's had a long trip,' said my father, taking a sip from his coffee. He watched the sun in the windows, the waitresses, the people standing in line to eat.

My mother studied me. 'You'll find someone else,' she said. My father rattled the cup in his saucer. My mother changed the subject. 'You'd probably like to get some rest,' she said.

I nodded.

'If you want to stay for a while, I can get you a job,' she said. My mother was high up in the ranks of a computer company.

'Maybe I'll stay for a while,' I said.

'Good,' she said, leaning back in her chair. She glanced at my father, who beamed.

I moved into my mother's guest room in her condo in Tarzana. The next day I started work building dictionary databases for court reporters. It was glorified word processing. I made eighteen thousand dollars that year, exceptionally good money for me.

I was sober now, my first concentrated campaign against chemical sloth and permanent childhood. Because I was the kind of person who drank to be someone else, I was not eager to form new friendships. As long as I stayed alone I felt I could stay sober. At night, like my mother, I brought work home with me. Anything to keep from falling back into the old hole. My mother stayed late every night at the office. When she finally came home, she liked to go out to dinner. We sat in a restaurant together and had trouble conversing. This was unusual for us; I believe it came from her guilt over leaving my father and my realization that I was exactly like him.

As a child growing up in San Diego, I had always despised the pervading smog and voracious anonymity of L.A. But living in L.A. wasn't so bad. It was a great place to be alone. On the weekends I drove to Santa Anita Racetrack, which lies like a polished English cobblestone village under the cool, dry blue shadows of the San Gabriel Mountains. Watching the horses fly around a track with money on them was the next best thing to getting high. There was nothing like those chilly winter L.A. mornings, and the crisp sound of your money flushing down the toilet. Occasionally my sister came with me. We were close growing up, good friends. To her misfortune, she respected and imitated me, and by nineteen she had already attended her first A.A. meeting. She was still a heavy drinker and occasional drug user. We were Wrecks Number Two and Three. My mother had gotten her a job at the computer firm three months before I'd limped in from Niagara Falls. She came with me six or seven times to the track — Hollywood Park when Santa Anita closed — and she never won a race in all the days we went. It takes a special talent to lose beyond any realm of probability, and it became a joke with us.

'Come on six!' she'd shout, taking a swig from her beer. 'Ya goddamn giraffe!' And we'd watch the thing stumble around the turn in fourth or seventh place. Usually the sky was dark by the time we left, the last race run under artificial light, the sweat of the horses like chrome as they flashed past, wrong numbers, tickets up in the air.

A guy named Bill befriended me at work. He talked exactly like Andy Griffith, smooth and cheerful and satisfied — sucking on his words like lemon drops. He had a big moon-pale face and soft curly brown hair. He was so friendly I worried about him. He came from a tiny town called Pineville, Louisiana. He seemed profoundly lonely, like most people who came to L.A. One night I invited him over to my sister's house for a game of Risk.

My sister lived in a ground floor apartment in El Segundo with a guy named Frank, a skinny wide-shouldered kid with a nose like Rocky Marciano, who worked as a technician in a histology lab. In the evenings, he and my sister drank. Like any good alcoholic couple, they played torpedo to each other's paddleboat out on the lake. They were both mean drunks. One night he might split her skull open, the next she might smash a chair over his head. When the cops showed up, my sister wanted to fight them. Once, she knocked a cop down while wearing handcuffs. (In the mornings they never remembered.)

My sister, a sweet child when she was not drinking, and always happy to have company unless it was the police at three in the morning, dragged the game of Risk down from the closet and began to set up the board on the dining-room table. Drinks were poured ('Just a cola for me, thanks,' I said). Bill surprised me by producing a bag of coke. He held up the gram of twinkling anesthetic and shook it at us like the magi with the magic gift.

'Just a cola for you,' he said.

I stared at it like an adolescent stares at the keys to the family Camaro. Every good boy deserves a favor, I thought.

'Do you want to toot it up?' he said.

'Better not,' I said.

'Come on,' he said. 'Just a couple of lines. It's all I've got…'

'Yeah, I know how it works,' I said.

'What the hell?' said my sister. 'Let's do it. Frank and I have some extra money.'

'I'm kind of trying to clean up my act,' I said weakly.

'You're so clean now you squeak,' said Frank.

'You haven't even gone out on a date since you've been in L.A.,' my sister added.

Haven't been out on a date since I quit doing drugs and alcohol, I wanted to clarify.

'All work and no play makes Jack a dull boy,' said Frank, reading my mind.

Maybe just this once, I thought. A short little spree, then right back to the straight and narrow. It would be good for me, I decided, a healthy break from the grind. I needed to loosen up, relax a little. I'd lost my spontaneity. I had nothing to show for being grown up and responsible. The old juices began to flow up into my jowls. I rubbed my palms together, suddenly eager to demonstrate my special knowledge of the arcane alchemy of freebasing cocaine, a trend that was about six months away from sweeping the country.

'Ever smoke it?' I said.

'No,' Bill said, wrinkling his brow.

'It's about twenty times better than sniffing.'

'Let's give it a try,' he said.

We hopped into my car and drove to a head shop, bought a glass pipe and some brass screens and a Pyrex vial. We stopped again at a liquor store and picked up a pint of Bacardi 151.

I cooked the coke when we got back, dropped half of it in the Pyrex vial with water and baking soda, brought it to a boil over a stove flame, then drew out the pure crystals by swirling a paper clip through the melted puddles that rose to the top. I laid the clumps of recrystallized cocaine on a saucer, then stuffed a dozen of the circular brass screens into the mouth of the glass pipe, dropped in a lump, dipped a Q-tip into the rum, lit it, and applied it to the lump.

The lump slowly vaporized, the chamber tumbled with smoke, and I hooped it in and passed it around. Vault of heaven. Love for all mankind. Potent and irresistible illusion of actually possessing a developed personality. Cheap treats for the weak.

'This is fantastic!' cried Wreck Number Three.

Both Frank and Bill nodded stern, jittery-eyed approval. Bill had suddenly become a chain smoker. Frank, the man who got so drunk every night he had been known to urinate into the curtains and one time even into the open refrigerator, took now social, even disinterested sips from his drink.

After the ecstasy of the first few hits, we settled down to the grim business of preventing the effects of the drug from wearing off, which is directly proportional to the amount of cash you have on hand.

Four grams and four hundred dollars later we were all slumped around the table like incinerated sheep, eyes rolling dismally in our heads. My sister poured herself a strong drink. Frank continued to hunt the table for escaped crumbs and periodically torch the lacy alkaloid patterns off the walls of the pipe chamber, trying to lift away the last euphoric tongues of drug-potent smoke. 'Look at me,' he said. 'You've turned me into a dope fiend!'

We started a game of Risk, which quickly grew pointless. It was getting late anyway, so Bill and I decided to leave. As we walked wordlessly to our cars in the lot, Bill stopped for a moment, jingling his pockets. 'I keep thinking I've left something behind.'

'Your grocery money,' I said.

He laughed.

'I'll see you at work tomorrow,' I said.

'Drive safely,' he said.

I climbed into my car and sat for a long time in the dark. It was a cool night and I started the engine and let it idle. Tomorrow I knew I would be in no shape to work. For a moment I thought about driving south toward Manhattan Beach and having a couple of drinks somewhere—never mind tomorrow—then I realized I was flat broke. On the radio I heard that the state of New York was requesting permission from the EPA to reopen Love Canal for habitation. I listened in disbelief. Then I thought of Charlene and felt so worthless and sad I turned off the radio and drove back home through the quiet streets to my mother's condo in Tarzana.

Where the Rain Belongs

for Cristina Dorado Hughes

AFTER THREE NIGHTS AT THE BROADWAY MOTEL OUT ON THE highway ($12.95 a night, color TV), a week in a forty-dollar-a-week First Street flophouse with free-running roaches, dying winos, and slender and wasted young homosexual men, two rumpled and freezing nights listening to the rain clatter against the roof of my car, and no luck finding an apartment or a job, I finally took to the streets of Eureka, California, on foot. I had just quit the drink and drug life cold and was starting all over, one more time. I had in my possession: a world globe, a sleeping bag, a box of clothes, a battered and thumb-worn 1969 *American Heritage Dictionary*, a brand-new copy of *Writer's Market*, an IBM Selectric type-writer, and my second novel, which unlike the first I knew would be a hit the minute I finished it.

Since the bottoms of the fishing and lumber industries had dropped out, the only people who lived in Eureka anymore were oil and acrylic painters from L.A., slim young men who had migrated north from San Francisco to die quietly and cheaply of AIDS, a few woolly misanthropic forestry students who attended Humboldt State University in Arcata six miles north, the stubbornly unemployed, the habitually poor, junkies on welfare, and the handful of fogdwellers like me, who, whether they had a dream about art or painted by numbers in the sewing room at twilight, had come to live here because it was cheap.

It rains a great deal in Eureka. This is after all a rain forest. The coastal redwoods create their own drizzly, prehistoric microclimate, sipping the fog off the sea like a root beer float. The sun rarely shows. The pulp mill out on Samoa Peninsula chugs up its fetid orange efflux twenty-four hours a day. I speak of the habitually poor. Eureka seemed to have more than its share. In my campaign for a room I hit some striking Third World pockets, with lawns like Mesozoic tar pits and toothless drifters asking *me* for money and mud-splattered porches crowded with soggy Naugahyde and busted Sears barbecues. At one house, a squat gothic relic that hadn't been painted since 1910, a mother of nine answered the door at high noon in a bathrobe. She appeared to be no more than twenty-seven. I showed her the newspaper. 'Do I have the right address?' I said.

'Oh, yes,' she said. 'Come in. I'm sorry I'm not dressed.' She didn't seem to be sorry that she was not dressed. The old house smelled of hay and soiled diapers and World War I breakfast grease. The children gathered all around me droopy-drawered and drippy-nosed and implored me with their eyes to become their father and recite something appropriately Dickensian.

The mother of nine, a blue-eyed one on her shoulder, showed me the rental room on the first floor, simply a bedroom with three chests of drawers and a bed into which a circus elephant had been dropped from the rafters. The curtains hung twisted in the stale air like nicotine-stained ghosts. The ceiling launched itself into the high lumber-tycoon darkness.

'Is there a kitchen?' I said.

'It's through there.'

'Where's the bathroom?'

'It's upstairs.'

'How many bathrooms are there?'

'There's only one.'

'For how many people?'

'Twelve. But it's never a problem,' she added hastily. The toilet flushed as if to underscore her remark. 'Do you want to see the kitchen?'

The children all stared up at me expectantly, their eyes beseeching me to park my carriage, stomp the snow off my boots, roll up my sleeves, and march into that kitchen to roast them a big goose with sloe fruit and farkleberries and saskatoons.

'I'm going to have a look at a few more places,' I said.

After a week of such forays and very tired of living in my car, I finally stumbled onto an old orange and green gingerbread Victorian, shiny-shingled, one spindle turret leaning in the mist. APT FOR RENT the sign in the curved bay window read. I walked up the steps and through the door into the vestibule to knock on the door of number one, which had the letters MGR scrawled in felt pen under the buzzer. A pregnant woman in her twenties answered. She seemed surprised to see me.

'Can I help you?' she said.

'Is the apartment still available?'

'Is it for you?' she said.

A short, angry-looking little man glared at me from the couch.

'Yes, for me.'

'Well, yes,' she said, as she continued to stare at me. A Heart record played in the background. 'You know who you look like?' she said.

'No, who?'

'Clark Kent.'

The angry little man, whose name turned out to be Del, sprang from the couch and swaggered across the room. You could have shot arrows from his sides the way he bowed his muscular arms. 'I'll show him the apartment,' he growled.

The apartment was ancient, unfurnished, high-ceilinged, and cold, with a huge bay window that looked out onto the street. I liked the big kitchen. I also enjoyed the absence of vermin and fruity smell of death. The promise of my own bathroom, even if the lion-footed bathtub was only large enough to drown a moth in, excited me.

'You can park around the side here,' said Del, showing me through the kitchen door, which led out onto a porch and a muddy yard. 'Be careful of that dog,' he said, pointing to a Siberian Husky chained to the wall and sitting calmly in the grass staring at us through its icy blue eyes. 'He's a killer. Don't get close to him.'

'What's his name?'

'Czar.'

'He's a good-looking dog,' I said.

'Meaner than a snake,' he said.

'Who's he belong to?'

Del jabbed a thumb into his sternum. 'Me.'

After I paid Del the Dog Lover $185 for a month's rent and a $125 deposit, he told me about the junkies on welfare who lived upstairs. 'Her old man owns this place,' he explained with a jerk of the head that I took to indicate his pregnant wife. 'I'd kick 'em out if this was my place. Section Eight, my ass. They give you any trouble you let me know...'

I had thirty-eight dollars to my name. I went to the store and bought groceries. I had to save five dollars for gas. I did not have enough money to buy cheese. But I was sober now, a nonsmoker, so I could live on very little. I worked for a while on my novel, a scathing social critique that inexplicably veered off into science fiction. Everything I wrote in those days veered off inexplicably into science fiction.

Later that afternoon I sat out on my kitchen porch for a while in the mist, and the dog and I stared at each other. Two children were playing nearby with a ball, which got away from them and rolled into the killer's territory. He stared at it, uninterested, classic killer profile. The children stared at it too, arms hanging dejectedly at their sides. There were four more such balls molding in his domain, lost forever, like gold coins in the lair of the legendary slobbering troll. The kids turned their attention to me. 'Don't look at me,' I said. 'I'm new here. I don't even know where the hospital is...'

There was no heat in the building except for a senile dwarf in the basement who rubbed two files together whenever the wind turned down from Nome, Alaska. Even though it was spring, Eureka is never a warm place, maybe two days in the summer over seventy-five. I slept on the floor in my sleeping bag and periodically woke with a start as something crashed or tumbled across my ceiling. The junkies who lived upstairs were on Peter Pan Time, not Pacific Standard. Long oceanic lulls were followed by squabbling followed by the sound of spoons clattering across the floor followed by the blasting of the stereo (no matter what time of night it was) followed by another long lull, then a sudden roaring burst of the theme song from *I Dream of Jeannie*. Occasionally, I heard a child howl or cry as if struck. Visitors clomped up and down the stairs at all hours, staying just long enough to say hello or perhaps exchange some item of sentimental importance, a baseball card or a slice of homemade German chocolate cake.

Meanwhile, I looked for a job, but there were simply none in Eureka. Finally I broke down and answered an ad that had been running in the newspaper since I'd arrived for a cook in Arcata, the little hippie-college town six miles north. The four owners of this restaurant had all been mistreated together as cooks and waitresses in another restaurant, so they'd pooled their money to open a restaurant of their own, complete with an unmanageably large menu. They tried hard to be hip and agreeable, but you could see fourteen-hour days, ignorant help, waitresses who stole from them, wily overcharging purveyors, two hundred forty-two items that had to be prepped fresh daily, ten-pound cans of tomatoes mysteriously exploding in the pantry, and cooks who didn't show up wearing them down. Soon they would have to make certain concessions to competitive restaurant reality and become more like the owners they had left behind, that or flee up into the hills to live in a teepee. They seemed happy to see me, probably because I wasn't fresh out of jail. How many responsible, competent, experienced people do you expect to come walking in your door to cook for minimum wage? I told them I could only cook part time because I was working on my novel, which I was convinced would be a commercial success any second. 'Cool,' said kitchen manager Dennis, a nonviolent macrobiotic dressed like a medieval peasant. He gripped my hand in a firm Grateful Dead handshake. 'Start tomorrow.'

On my second week of living in the green and orange gingerbread Victorian, a pot of pinto beans simmering aromatically on the stove, I heard a kid bang through the vestibule door and shout on his way up the stairs: 'Are you COOKING something, Mom?' A moment later, he was back down the stairs, knocking on my door.

I answered to find a small, thin, wide-eyed boy with big pink ears sticking out from the bald sidewalls of his punk-rock haircut. He wore grass-stained orange bellbottoms, an oversized blue polo shirt, and black mud-encrusted Goodwill oxfords. He looked to be about eight years old. He had a cast on his arm with a happy face painted on it. 'Are you the new neighbors?' he said.

'Yes, I am.'

'The people who lived here before got kicked out.'

'Is that right?'

'Yeah.' He arched his eyebrows at me. 'They didn't pay no rent.'

'I usually pay my rent.'

'What's your name?' he demanded.

I told him.

'I'm Henry,' he said in a tuneful little voice, extending his good hand. 'I live upstairs.' He swung his cast up to indicate the junkie apartment. I shook his hand, which was soft and small as a mouse.

'How'd you break your arm?' I asked him

'Fell off my bike.'

'How long you have to wear the cast?'

'Eight more weeks.'

'Itch?'

'Yeah. Oh, yeah. I scratch down there with a hanger sometimes. Do you cook?'

'Yes, I do.'

'It smells good. What is it?'

'Beans,' I said. I considered inviting him in, then thought better of it.

'Where'd you learn how to cook?'

'Just picked it up along the way.'

'My mom don't cook,' he said dolefully.

'What about your dad?'

'My dad's dead.'

'Who's that up there with your mom?'

'That's her boyfriend, Terrance.' He pronounced the name with a snarl.

I nodded, feeling vaguely depressed. He pressed his lips together.

'I gotta go,' he said, whirling and banging back out the vestibule door.

The next night when the stereo blasted on at three in the morning, I walked up the stairs and knocked on the door. A long-nosed corpse in a porkpie hat answered. He squinted as if trying to place me.

'Can you please turn your stereo down? It's 3 a.m.'

'You a cop?'

'No. I live downstairs.'

'Oh, yeah,' he said. 'Sure thing, man,' he said, and closed the door.

Every night when I came home from the restaurant, I'd park in the muddy grass alongside the house and the Vicious

Killer Dog chained up with nothing to do but look fierce would look at me fiercely. He was so fierce he didn't even bark. I began to bring him scraps from the restaurant. After the checks started coming in I began buying him canned dog food. His masters visited him once a week for as long as it took to fill a plastic pan with dried dog chow that would sit against the wall under the eaves and soak up rain. I gave Czar a can every morning, chucking his cornmeal sludge off into the bushes. I had to be careful to maintain the chain's length distance. He watched me with the cold murderous calm of the predator, waiting for his chance to pounce. One sunny morning after feeding him I reached out without thinking to pet him. He thumped his tail all around. I patted his head and scratched him between the ears. He lowered his head and closed his eyes as I rubbed, pushing his head up into my hand and wagging his tail some more. I felt like a fool. He was about as mean as I was.

Terrance, the needle-nosed junkie in the porkpie hat, seemed to think I was funny. Ever since I had gone upstairs to politely ask him to turn his stereo down, he had gone out of his way to turn his stereo up. He grinned at me yellow-toothed in the foyer, flicking his head up in a smart-alecky street challenge and greeting me as 'partner' and 'bro.' One rainy afternoon he banged through the vestibule door while I was typing and over the objections of his girlfriend ('Be quiet, Terry, can't you hear he's typing…?') shouted at the cracks in my door: 'I don't give a damn, I'll punch him in the face.'

There are times, especially in poor neighborhoods with people who have no understanding of society other than what they learned getting their diapers changed, when you must show that you are not only not afraid, but eager to engage in violence. And Terrance was not physically imposing. He couldn't have weighed more than one hundred forty pounds soaking wet with a syringe in his arm. I don't think he ate more than seven or eight Twinkies a day. I thought I could probably pick him up and plant him in the yard. But I didn't move from the table. I told myself that even though the death penalty might be useful in some cases, no benefit would ever come from punishing the dead.

That very night, as if Fate had thrown two bugs into a jar and would not take the lid off until they were locked in mortal combat, an orange circle appeared in my living room ceiling and began to spread like the rings of Jupiter. Soon a smelly spout of rusty water sprang from its center. I set a pan under the leak and ran up the stairs. I heard clucking and spoon-clattering inside. 'Open up,' I cried, pounding on the door. 'Something is leaking into my living room...'

Finally the door opened a crack, Terrance poked his skinny nose through. His eyes were purplish and heavy, like grapes at half-mast. 'Oh, it's you,' he sneered drowsily. 'What do you want?'

'My ceiling is leaking.'

'So?'

'It's coming from up here.'

He squinted at me sulkily. I saw by the muscles in his pale forearm that he was about to close the door in my face.

'It's coming from up HERE,' I repeated.

Terrance regarded me with his sagging, impenetrably dark and plantlike eyes. I was about to wedge my foot in the door when Del the Dog Lover, arms bowed, came charging past me up the stairs to throw the door aside, almost knocking both me and Terrance down.

'What the fuck is going on up here, Terry?' he shouted. 'You jamming up the pipes again?'

Terrance gave a languid, resigned blink. His toothless, glassy-eyed girlfriend sat like a freshly killed rabbit, licking her cracked lips on the sagging brown couch. The little place was hot as a gerbil cage and swimming with the miserable smell of neglect. The floor was strewn with junk-food wrappers, crusty boots, and paper plates with nacho cheese and ketchup stains. An electric heater buzzed in the corner, its bright orange coils singeing the last few atoms of oxygen out of the air.

'You live here free, man,' said Del, 'and we all put up with your shit. That don't mean you get to trash the place. I warned you about flushing needles down the toilet.'

'I hate your guts,' replied Terrance dreamily.

'You talk to me like that again,' said Del, as he moved toward the bathroom, 'I'll knock your junkie ass out the window.'

'I wasn't talking to you,' he said, staring at me with a gentle loathing that broke into a tranquil yellow smile that seemed to float by itself all alone in the room.

I must've written my first novel one hundred thirty-five times before I finally slam-dunked it into the trash. It doesn't matter how many times you write something if it isn't any good. But I still believed an article I had read in *Writer's Market* that said that rewriting was the key to success. I also believed in many other silly things that I had read in *Writer's Market* or that people with no experience or qualification had told me, including my recently long-held but abandoned aesthetic view of the world that required writers to be sots and libertines who shunned opportunity and died young falling drunk off yachts or getting in car accidents on the way back from funerals in El Centro.

But I was rewriting one afternoon, hammering away on my IBM Selectric in that misguided, transient, isolated, and painfully sober period of my life that I can only describe as 'The Diligent Typing Era,' when I heard screaming out back. *The dog has finally savaged a child*, I thought, and bolted up and out the kitchen door to salvage what I could. Czar was on his back, tangled up in his chain, legs drawn in, yelping as if someone were hitting him with a stick. A crowd of children, including Henry, had gathered, but no one would get close. The pregnant manager came bustling around the corner and crouched to touch him but he lunged at her in long vicious snaps. When I came down the porch stairs and knelt to the dog's side, the gallery behind me fell into a stunned silence. I ran my fingers through his coat, pressed in on his stomach. I couldn't figure out what might be wrong with him. Pretty soon, though, he climbed up on his feet and shook himself off, panting and limping in a little circle.

The pregnant manager stared at me incredulously.

'Maybe he got stung by a bee,' suggested Henry.

The manager gawked at me another moment longer. 'He let you touch him,' she said.

'He probably got stung by a bee,' I said.

She shook her head at me and went back inside. The children faded away too, all except Henry. We stayed with the dog. 'Pet him if you want,' I said. 'He'd like that.'

'No,' he said.

'Nothing to be afraid of. Look, just a dog. Made-up stories.' I petted the dog to show him. Czar wagged his tail. 'You see?'

Henry wasn't quite up for petting him, though. The way Czar had lunged at his own master didn't help matters much, though if Henry himself had been tied by his neck to a wall to sit in the mud and be ignored entirely for the rest of his life with nothing to look forward to but a pan of soggy corn stink once a week, he might've understood.

Then again, I wondered, how much better was Henry's life than Czar's? He was not a healthy child. I asked him what he had for breakfast. 'A Pop Tart,' he said.

'But they feed you at school?'

'Yeah,' he said.

'Got your cast off, I see.'

'Yup.'

'How's it feel?'

He flexed his fingers and pushed out his lips. 'Good,' he said.

'That's good. You hungry?'

'Yeah,' he said.

'Hold on a sec.' I went back inside and heated him a bowl of beef stew. I made sure to feed him outside to keep the neighbors from talking.

Henry went after the stew like Czar would've, finishing it in about eight seconds flat. 'That was good,' he said, licking the spoon. 'What was it?'

'Beef stew. You want another bowl?'

'No,' he said. 'Could I have the recipe?'

I wrote it down for him, feeling a little sick as I imagined him turning it over to his mother. 'Can you cook this for me, mom?' 'Sure, honey, I'll cook it for you (applying flame to spoon and tightening the tourniquet on her arm with her teeth), just as soon as I cook this...'

AFTER WORK ONE AUTUMN NIGHT I DROVE UP ALONGSIDE THE crumbling orange and green gingerbread mansion and turned off the headlights. Czar danced on his hind legs at the end of his chain, smiling. I was happy to see him too. I had a couple of bones for him from the restaurant. I sat with him for a while and watched him contentedly chew his bones. This gave me none of the usual satisfaction. He was a healthy young dog, and the fact that he could move no more than six feet in any direction had been gnawing at me for a long time. I had never once seen him off that chain.

After a while I stood up and let him off the chain. He nearly yanked me to the ground. I secured the loop on his collar and dragged him to the car. He strained against me, all muscle, choking to get free. I stuffed him into the car, and he jumped all around frantically, bounding from the front to the back to the front again. After a minute he settled himself into the passenger seat and gave me a quick glance of giddy disbelief. I started the car and backed out and headed for the beach. Czar shoved his head out the open window, prancing on the seat, snorting and rearing and smelling the air.

Clam Beach was twenty miles north. I parked down in the empty lot. Not a soul out. It was midnight. There were no lights for miles. A heavy canopy of clouds shut out the moon and stars. Czar was in a near frenzy to get free. I opened the car door and he shot out into the darkness and was gone.

I assumed for a minute that he would return. He was smart enough to understand the risk I had taken, the trust I had invested in him. We had this bond. We had been through a great deal together. I had bought him canned food. I strolled down the horseshoe-shaped beach, feigning calm. The tide was out. I could hear but not see the surge of frigid, rugged surf in the distance. The sand was cold and heavy under my feet and gave up the faint scent of rust and smoke and sleep. The first thin black shell of sea fizzed up the hard pack to touch the tips of my shoes. I looked left, then right. No trace of that dog. I called his name, then listened, only hearing the endless snatch and drop of the waves running in.

A sense of doom began to seep into my bowels. I walked for half an hour, north, then south again. I paced the road above the parking lot, yelling his name. I began to formulate what I would tell his lousy masters. I owed them a new dog. Of course, if I didn't tell them, I thought, or if I set up a cardboard cutout of Czar, they might never notice. I called out his name. With a whoosh the waves flattened down onto the sand.

Well, maybe for the best, I decided at last. I would pay for his freedom, but freedom for how long, I wondered? A Siberian Husky on the rainy desert beaches of northern California. And how 'free' is a domesticated animal without a master or a home? Again I called his name long and loudly, and then started the long march of defeat back to the car.

When I opened my car door he came out of nowhere, grazing the backs of my legs and leaping in nonchalantly to take his place in the passenger's seat, and giving me a foxy, glittery-eyed look that read something like: *What are you waiting for, Bub, let's hit the road.*

I should've stolen him then. Hit the road, Bub. I could've easily moved to Crescent City or some other place just as cheap and dreary as Eureka. I had always wanted a dog. Czar and I would've made a great team. No entity but a six-foot chain and an empty law would've been broken. Instead I mumbled to myself a bromide about the categorical obligation of humans to moral standards and drove him back to the green and orange Victorian and put him on the end of his chain. He was wet and sandy and smelled smoky and

free. I pretended that I had done something noble. He
plopped down on the ground and took up a bone.

SITTING IN THE CAR ACROSS THE STREET WAITING FOR THE
rain to let up one dark and drab Thursday afternoon, I
watched Terrance the junkie stroll outside, swinging his
arms. He lit up a cigarette, then turned and reached into
my mailbox and groped around like a cat with its paw in
the goldfish bowl. I started to get out of the car, but saw
Henry coming down the street, heading home from school.
He wore a cheap blue plastic jacket with a grease stain on
the arm. He held his weak arm up in front of him, as if he
were checking the time. His punk haircut was plastered
and dripping. He swiped his foot through a puddle. When
he saw Terrance up on the porch he slowed. Terrance tossed
his cigarette into the grass and gestured for the boy to come
out of the rain. Henry climbed the wooden stairs. Terrance
leaned down, clasped the back of Henry's neck, and spoke
in his ear. Then he pointed his finger and struck him in
the face with the back of his hand. Henry opened the foyer
door and tore up the stairs.

That evening Henry knocked on my side door. He stood
draggled and dripping out on the stoop. I had never let him
inside before. There was already tension about my feeding
him. I had not yet realized that by trying to help him, I was
only making things worse. 'Come in, Henry,' I said. 'What
have you been doing, walking around in the rain?'

'Yeah, kinda.'

A dirty puddle began to form at his feet. 'Let me get you a towel. What happened there?' I said, pointing at his swollen eye.

He gave a little shrug. 'Got hit by a ball at school.'

'Oh. You OK?'

'Yeah.'

'You hungry?'

'Nah.'

'You want a Coke?'

'OK.'

I got him a Coke. He slung the towel around his shoulders like a boxer and toured my apartment. There wasn't much to look at, piles of discarded typing paper, my nest of blankets and sleeping bag in the corner. A Goodwill dining table with an electric typewriter on it. He spun the world globe and said: 'What do you do down here anyway?'

'Eat, sleep, that kind of thing.'

'I mean all that typin'. You're always typin'.'

'I'm writing a book.'

He sat down on my only chair and took a swig from his cola. He squinted and touched his swollen eye. 'What's it about?'

'It's a social critique.'

He stared at me.

'With violent clowns in it,' I added.

'Oh,' he said.

I was about to expand on my rosy literary future — as a matter of fact, I'd been waiting for a reply from a big-time

New York agent, whose name I had gotten out of the back of *Writer's Market* — when I heard the upstairs door squeak open. Henry's mother called blearily down the stairs.

The boy and I shared a moment of apprehensive silence. 'You'd better get going,' I said at last. 'Your mom doesn't like you down here.'

'My mom don't care,' he said.

I went to bed early that night, pulled the sleeping bag up over my head, and listened to the wind from Nome, Alaska, carving down through the crags and niches of the icebergs floating out on Humboldt Bay. About two o'clock, the junkies woke me up with a clatter of spoons. I heard the toilet flush. Then I heard Henry's voice and then Henry crying. I put on a jacket and a hat and paced the room. I stared at the violent clowns on the sheet of paper in the typewriter. Then I went out to visit Czar, who was asleep in the soft rain. When he heard the porch boards squeak he looked up and thumped his tail at me.

When I had saved up enough money I began looking for apartments downtown. I wanted to be closer to the store and the library and the post office, and also to get out from under the junkies. I was also thinking about selling my car. There were plenty of apartments downtown, but most of them were too expensive. One day I answered an ad at a security apartment building on H Street. The lady who ran the place, a wacky fascist with a telescope in her living room window (she claimed to work for the police) said there would be a studio opening at the beginning of the month. Two hundred a month. I thought a complex run by a female version of Hermann Göring would at least be quiet, so I gave her a holding fee and headed back home. Turning the corner I came upon Terrance fishing around in my mailbox again. I was certain he had stolen the positive reply from the big-time New York agent. He grinned when he saw me. He had a piece of mail in his hand.

'Is that mine?' I said.

'No, it's mine.'

'I thought I saw you with your hand in my mailbox.'

'No, man, you didn't see right. You oughta get your glasses fixed.'

'Could I look at that piece of mail?'

'It's mine.'

'I just want to look at it.'

'Fuck you,' he said. 'It's mine.'

I tried to hit him in the face. He ducked and we locked up. 'You piece of shit,' I growled at him. 'You've been stealing my mail.'

'I'll kill you,' he answered in a hoarse and depraved whisper that smelled like an old man smoking cigars in an outhouse. We grappled and grunted and stumbled around on the old porch boards. My record in street fights, almost all of them compiled as a child, was four wins, one hundred eighteen losses, and thirty-three run-like-hells. But Terrance was not a fighter either. He tried to kick me in the crotch with his muddy boot, but I caught his heel and gave him a shove that sent him cartwheeling with a rough oath over the rail and into the muck of the dead irises below.

Terrance floundered in the soup of the flowerbed, a bitter and indignant smirk playing over his lips. Finally he lifted himself, pushed off an elbow, and climbed up shakily, half-dipped in mud. He gave me a grim and nauseated grin, dropped my piece of mail on the ground, retrieved his porkpie hat, and slouched away around the corner.

I walked down the stairs and picked up my piece of mail, a Kentucky Fried Chicken coupon book addressed to 'Occupant.'

A month later, I was living in a second-floor apartment in Ms. Hermann Göring's Security Apartment Building and Police Auxiliary downtown. It was no less quiet and no better place to type, but it had a row of beautiful arched windows that took up the entire western wall and offered a splendid view of the Samoa pulp mill and its backdrop ocean sky like a piece of angel food cake drenched in orange juice. I sold my car and quit the job at the restaurant. Ms. Göring hired me to paint apartments and serve eviction notices, one free month's rent for each apartment painted, fifteen bucks for an eviction notice successfully served. I began another novel, which started off well but then kangarooed off again somehow into the vast billabong of science fiction. The rain splattered across the high, arched windows and I watched the haggard, moribund young men in their red plaid shirts shambling desolately down the walks. Oh, I think that was another of those miserable times. But every week or so, I would cross town to go visit my old friend, Czar. I usually went at night, so as not to be seen. He was always happy to see me, dancing on his hind legs at the end of his chain. I would toss his foul-smelling corn sludge off into the bushes and fill his bowl with something good to eat. But then one night, he was gone too. It was the end of fall, getting cold, his kind of weather, and I came around the corner to find only the chain lying in the grass. The hook that had held him was still intact. Someone had let him off. I kicked one of the molding plastic balls out into the street and walked the mile and a half back home.

Never and Nowhere

I LEAVE THE LEANING PHONE BOOTHS OF LOUISVILLE, KENTUCKY, and the thick green twilight and the slow-blossoming dogwoods (and all those hookers circling my downtown motel like tranquil sharks in their tan leather jackets and parasols), and I head west on the bus with nine hundred eighty-four dollars and some roast beef sandwiches and some bananas and a bag of trail mix and the usual doubt and the usual set of diminishing expectations. For twenty years I've had a vision of the ideal place. I've tried to explain the place but I can't. It is something like nowhere but not a ghost town. It is alive. It is not the vision of a televangelist: *Leave It To Beaver* with a cop on every corner. Neither is it some apparition of the future: twenty-four-hour abortion and free milkshakes for the poor. It's a place just as free as New York City, but there are no hookers circling my motel room like tranquil sharks in their tan leather jackets and parasols, and it's quite possible I can't buy liquor on Sundays. Nobody seems to understand this place. I know it exists. People say: *You oughta go to Elvis in Velveetaland, they got a dog track up there*; or: *You oughta try Florida (or Hawaii or Bermuda), the weather's real nice.* Or: *You know, they got good jobs down around the Gulf.* Nobody listening, people only telling me the place *they* want to live, giving me *their* version of paradise: eighteen bucks an hour and a short winter and a dog track on the edge of town.

When I say the word 'Iowa' to someone sitting next to me on the bus, they understand immediately and nod their heads and think, though they have never been there before, corn, flat, pig, dull. 'What do you want to go there for?' But the bus glides through the rain and mist and darkness and into the setting sun. And soon the land has smoothed down to a long rolling green and the cities have given up their grip. The sky seems to be getting bluer and the people seem to be getting friendlier. Even the restaurant coffee tastes like someone sneaked chocolate liqueur into it. I try not to get my hopes up. I wonder how everybody could be wrong.

The destination on my ticket reads Waterloo, population 66,000, but Waterloo is not right, not even close; it's a littered, peeling, dirty little town. As usual, the name of the city has tricked me. I've been to every tourist flock, every hot spot, every fashion center, every city with the second name of Springs or Beach or Falls, and I still haven't learned that picking a city from a map is like picking a girl from the phone book. I don't even need to get off the bus.

So I go to Independence, which I passed about twenty miles back and the fare is only five dollars, and I like it all right but I can't find a place to live. The motel is twenty-six a night. I leave after three days. In Cedar Falls I stay at the Blackhawk Hotel for a week for eighty bucks, and get groceries down the street at the Safeway and watch the NBA play-offs and eat Spaghetti-O's right out of the can, but Cedar Falls isn't it either. The guy at the desk in the lobby of the Blackhawk Hotel, which also serves as the bus depot, tells me northeast Iowa is the place to go, Oelwein, Decorah. He thought for a long time that I wanted to go to Dubuque because they have a dog track in Dubuque, but I finally explained to him that a place with a dog track is the *last* place I want to go. I am looking for a place where *nothing* is happening. *Nowhere*, man. He had to think on that for a while because most people in Iowa grew up in a place exactly as I have described and dreamt all their lives of getting the hell out to a town with a little sin in it, like Dubuque. But now he's on my wavelength. He tells me with assurance that I'll like Decorah. I am thinking west for whatever reason, Fort Dodge and then Sioux City, and if that doesn't work then up into South Dakota, just forget Iowa, but there is something about the way he says it, the look in his eyes, that steady Midwestern conviction, that makes me say, even though the ticket is twenty dollars more, all right, give me a ticket to Decorah.

The bus drops me off in Decorah and whooshes away and that little office that doubles as the depot is already closed. Across the street on the other side of the highway are the red plastic roofs, the Dairy Queen and the KFC, the Hardee's and the Wal-Mart and the Pizza Hut, and the bile rises from my throat up into my eyes. I could be in Colorado Springs or Tampa Bay or Bakersfield. I could be anywhere or everywhere. What's the point of taking all these highways, getting so far away, spending my last few dollars, when the world is just one big franchise loop and wherever I go, no matter how far I travel, the bus always dumps me off right back where I started?

So I sit on my little purple bag I've had for nine years that's stuffed with grease-stained clothes. It's like a big pillow I can sit on in the late spring, late afternoon, in this red-plastic-northeast-corner-of-Iowa-village after the bus office has closed on me, and I think: I've been let down once more. No point in staying here. I'm moving on, east or north. That place that I described to the guy behind the desk at the Blackhawk exists, but I'm the only one who can find it. No one else can give it to me. If someone else has found it, it belongs to him. And I think: I'm just going to sit here all night because I don't want to spend thirty dollars for a bed and some TV shows with Pizza Hut commercials and a shower and some perfumed soap chips and all the time worried about checkout at 11 a.m. I can eat for ten days on thirty dollars. Thirty bucks will buy a lot of cream cheese sandwiches.

So I just sit there steamed on my stuffed purple bag with the broken zipper and another bag to my left, a handbag (that smells like the aftershave of an Air Force cadet) that I found in a Las Vegas dumpster, where I also found a Gideon's Bible with the Lord's Prayer underlined in pencil. I've got that Bible and all my cooking tools and a travel alarm and a few other things in the green dumpster handbag that smells like the aftershave of an Air Force cadet, and I have six hundred twelve dollars and I think: I am just going to sit here all night. I don't care how cold it gets, and when the bus comes in the morning I'll climb aboard and say, 'So long Iowa — everything they said about you was true.'

But I haven't seen the town yet, the real town. It lies over the hill. And I wonder only for a moment if it might yet be the place. This is just the highway, where the tourists come blazing through on their way to Broadway plays and oral sex. So I sit there for a long time and just sit there and the traffic streaks by as if someone has sped up time and forgot to tell me about it, and the sun sinks and glitters and catches the drifting pollen from the trees and I think, well, I've got some squashed cream cheese sandwiches and a peach and some peanuts and I don't really want to sit out here all night. I have six hundred twelve dollars and one day I'll be dead and it won't make a bit of difference if I spent thirty dollars on that motel room — so I pick up my stupid bags and trudge back up the highway to the nearest motel, which has an indoor pool and a restaurant, and I pay the thirty bucks and buy a newspaper in the lobby.

My room has no windows and someone has stolen the painting off the wall (there are just the plastic studs), and I wonder why someone would steal a motel painting. I watch the TV and it makes me feel empty, so I turn it off and open the paper and look through the ads and the rentals are cheap; there are a few jobs (two cooking), so I decide maybe I will just stay here in this plastic taco village for awhile. I am sore of traveling and down to five hundred eighty-four dollars, and with breakfast in the morning at the restaurant that will be five hundred seventy-nine, and a bus ticket will make it five twenty-seven, and pretty soon I'm in a homeless shelter playing cards with a drug addict named Vic.

I give one of the rentals a call, a place for $160 a month, and though the place is already rented, the woman wants to talk to me with an open kind of breath-mint freshness. She isn't lonely, just friendly. It feels like the AT&T people have spliced me into 1952 for a minute: I can smell the gladiolas and hear the fizzing of Coca-Cola and the riffle of bridge cards and I know she is whipping up some fabulous cheese and wienie recipe for the Pillsbury Bake-Off. I tell her, with a trace of weariness and childlike hope in my voice, that I am just passing through but I would like to find a place to stay for a while, and she says the same thing that the guy behind the desk at the Blackhawk Hotel said: 'Oh, you'll like Decorah.' She gives me this sudden sense that I actually belong somewhere, that maybe I was kidnapped from here long ago, stolen right out from under my mother's ironing board and forced to go to high school in California, where they gave me drugs and told me the world was coming to an end, but now I have found my way back, stumbled back somehow against all odds like Rover after he fell off the waterfall in Yellowstone Park, and for no reason other than faith, a faith no different than any other faith (I have to believe because that is why I came), I believe her.

There are more ads, but now I want to see the town; there is just a little light left in the sky, so I wander back down the highway past the bus station and start up the hill. The world is wicked when it all becomes one thing, when it all looks like the Coco's in El Paso, when the satellite takes photos from a distance and the earth has a red plastic roof on it. I find myself muttering. I wonder if Jesus will return. I HOPE that space aliens abduct me, and all the while I'm coming down the hill toward the little Iowa town. There are big bluffs all around and the place called Decorah is nestled into them, a little town of about eight thousand, spread out in a drowsy puddle of melted-butter light. I see a meeting hall called the Sons of Norway. I pass a small diner with a sign in the window that says 'Homemade Pie.' The time has slowed. I look back over my shoulder once. The windows of the little houses flood with the melted-butter light. The big green maples cut purple lacework patterns across my chest. The sky is as gold as a Byzantine dome, and the birds are gliding and diving and making slow backstrokes through the air. Two little boys come flying at me down the hill in their soapbox cars.

I stop and catch my breath for a moment. I wonder how anyone ever found this place or how it was made or how they stayed so far off the beaten path, and how they kept from being devoured by the Wal-Mart and the Pizza Hut that crouch like wolves at the edge of town. The people smile at me knowing that I'm not a criminal; if I were, I would have moved to Las Vegas long ago. Then I wander back to the motel. It is already dark along the highway. I take out a sandwich and eat it as a monk would, thinking not of appetite or sustenance but of the noumenal essence of cream cheese. Then I go down and sit by the indoor pool with a sort of warm brandy glow in my chest because I knew I would find this place. It was out here waiting for me all along.

In the morning I make one more phone call about a one-bedroom apartment, $185, no utilities. The landlord, Gary, a schoolteacher and a Lutheran, says come on out. He shows me the place, and I tell him my story: 'Just looking for a place. I travel pretty light...' and he says, 'That's fine, if you don't have the money for the deposit, you can just give it to me later.' But I pay it all to him gratefully. I should give him all my money. I feel I owe it to him for playing the part of the 1952 Lutheran schoolteacher landlord in the town where I was kidnapped out from under the ironing board while my mother was watching King Kong and dreaming of winning the Pillsbury Bake-Off.

'I'll see if I can get you some furniture,' he says.

'No, that's all right,' I say. 'Please don't go to the trouble. I'll find some things. That's the way I always do it.'

'What are you going to sleep on?'

'I'll get a bed or something eventually.'

'I've got a mattress,' he says, 'just sitting around, and a little table and a chair. I'll bring them over...'

My apartment is large, with a cement shower and parti-colored shag carpeting and a nice kitchen. I lie on the mattress with the green blanket I bought at Penney's for eight dollars and forty-nine cents. I have one hundred eighty-one dollars left, rent paid, a little food in the fridge, utilities turned on, table and chair, and an architecture book I borrowed from the library. The sun hanging in the windows seems to be stuck. My Christian landlord probably pointed at it and said, 'Stop for a minute while my new tenant, who travels light and who has had such a hard life because he was kidnapped at a young age, gets himself adjusted to this new town.'

The job-hunting, even in this golden dozing Norwegian fairy-tale village, is not easy. I follow the ads and get turned down by a pizza place called Happy Joe's, then a janitorial outfit called Pioneer, then a chicken-processing plant and a factory that makes ice chests and a factory that makes fishing lures. It goes like this for a few days. Restaurants give me a closer look and the woman at the diner called Mom's says, 'Try us in two weeks.' Hard to slip into a place so fixed and slow-paced, but the people are cheerful, slightly overweight and ruddy-cheeked from the prosperity of agriculture and God, and they shake my hand encouragingly, as if to say everything is going to work out just fine.

Then I'm back in the one-bedroom apartment for $185 a month, and I cook a pot of pinto beans with onions and garlic and listen to the clock radio that I bought at the hardware store for $14.95. I spin the dial and listen to the people talk, like neighbors standing out on their porches, and the DJs play old songs like 'Twelfth of Never' and '*Vaya con Díos*,' as if nothing has changed here for forty years.

Then the twilight comes, and suddenly there are these puffballs raining by the window in the golden twilight, and the kids outside have come to ride their homemade soapbox derby cars down the hill out front. They scream and shout and laugh, and the ringing of their voices and their laughter as they fly downhill in their wooden boats is so beautiful it is like being stabbed in the heart by the one who made you.

Soon it is dark and the children have gone home. A patch of warm, apricot light on the wood paneling flickers on the wall from the streetlight through the curtains; I watch it not only because I am bored with my architecture book, but also because there is something fascinating about light. I know that light is somehow the source from which everything arose and to which everything will return. Not knowing how I know won't prevent me from watching the light. I watch it like the dog watches its master, and I listen to the radio and lie on the mattress. It gets late and slowly, without knowing it, I drift off to sleep.

In the morning I have eggs and a shower, and I venture out to look for that job. At the unemployment office (which they call 'Job Service' in Iowa), the emphysemic receptionist with the cherry-frosted goldfish lips and the helmet of red hair, nervous and incompetent, squints at me. 'What do you want?' she says. 'Oh, yeah. Subway is hiring today.'

I fill out an application and sit down with about eight other applicants. Subway lies at the edge of town with all the other red plastic roofs. The owner sits back behind a Job Service partition holding interviews and bellows in a mellifluous baritone like the father of all fathers: 'Subway's the fastest-growing franchise in America.' A pair of pretty young college-girl twins from Sri Lanka are here for the interview. He pronounces it Sarry Lanka. 'That used to be Ceylon,' he says. 'Not many people know where Sarry Lanka is, not one in ten, but I'm in the travel business.' The twin sisters from Sarry Lanka smile at him. 'You all have such beautiful smiles,' he says.

The guy sitting next to me has been released from jail for the afternoon to apply at Subway. He wants a full-time job making sandwiches so he doesn't have to spend so much time in jail. He's served four months, has eight to go. He's in for breaking a TV over a guy's head in a bar. He tells me he's from France, so he can sympathize with the Sarry Lanka twins. He's trying to pick one up while the other is in for the interview. He refers to his sentence as 'when I got in trouble,' as though he might be a little boy and the State is his Dad. He seems to be proud of planting a TV on someone's head. He recounts the event in colorful detail, and it appears to impress the Sarry Lanka twins.

The Subway owner asks questions like: What do you like to do? Do you like sports? What are your plans after you get out of school? He has a long list of summer camp questions. What does this have to do with making sandwiches? I leave the office after five people have gone in before me. I will do anything, of course, I am in no bargaining position. I have ninety-one dollars left and very little pride. But I am a little old for a funny hat and summer camp questions.

Church bells ring, 11 a.m. It rained this morning, but I was asleep, blanket over my head. It is cloudy now; maybe it will rain some more. There is a bumblebee's nest somewhere up in the ceiling or in the wall, and the bumblebees slip out every now and then, float down into the room. I try to figure out where they are coming from, how they get in, but they just descend, one every day or so, float and bump around the room. I try to catch them and help them back outside. One day a bumblebee is hovering around and just drops straight into the beef stew. By the time I fish him out he is a goner. Another day, just out of bed, I step on one and he stings my foot and I pound the little bastard into the carpet with the bottom of my shoe.

At last I find a job. Gordon from New Jersey brought the diner of his boyhood youth all the way from New Jersey and planted it in Iowa, and he's going to open it in two weeks. He found the town working on the railroad, stumbled on it like I did, and he knows nothing about running a restaurant, he only knows about the diner of his youth in the town of his dreams ('You'll like Decorah,' says the decal in the window) with the songs of his youth playing on the jukebox. He thinks I am a clown when I come through the door, just one more clown who wants to dunk French fries and get home early to experiment with my new rubber-ball nose, but I have cooked in about fifteen places. After I talk with him a while and show him my job history and my tools, he wrings my hand as if I am an obstetrician who has just announced it is a boy, ten pounds two ounces.

So I work in the diner and business is good and I pay the rent and live in the town of Decorah with the safeness and the decency and the churches and the unlocked bicycles and the melted-butter light that fades into comfort like a long afternoon in the curtains of your great-aunt. I meet a girl and eventually begin to have feelings for her. She is an editor of an archaeology magazine, and although she makes thirteen dollars an hour, she works in the evenings as a waitress at the diner. I look forward to the nights she works. I like everything about her, the tilt of her head and the bright glints in her dark eyes and her pride and the way her breath comes up and the way she loves to be alive but doesn't really know what to do with it, which is why she is waiting tables in the evenings in the diner of Gordon's youth and not out instead with her boyfriend, who is a bum. Maybe I could save her from the bum…well, that's a pretty stale story. She is with the bum for a good reason, and whatever dance they are doing, I am not a part of it. Pretty soon, I'll have to be moving along. I couldn't fall for her anyway. Would she come with me? Would she live on a bus? Would she give up her career and her pretty boyfriend for part-time jobs and a pot of beans and bumblebees falling out of the ceiling?

I live in Decorah almost a year because I want to see all the seasons, and the town in snow and the children growing up and the purple dapple of the shade trees and the drunks going home and the juvenile delinquents angry at storefront windows and the pain in someone's eyes when they are lost or when they just don't know anymore. The seasons seem long and some of the nights are even longer, but there are the books and there on the wall is the apricot light out of which I arose and to which I will return, and there is the radio and the thoughts of the girl; and then, when spring comes and the snow is going away, I would like to stay because this is my place now, my home. I fought hard to find it. I have come a long way and looked a long time. But this is not my place. Because this place will never be my place; it will always be the next place. How long will it take me to figure that out?

Gary the Lutheran schoolteacher landlord seems sorry to see me go. He never doubted me from the beginning. Simple trust. I pack up all my junk, leave the mattress and the table, leave the pots and pans, leave the travel alarm because it's stuck at four o'clock. I get everything in two bags, the nine-year-old purple bag that I bought in Niagara Falls and the green handbag I found in a Las Vegas dumpster. I shake hands all around. Gary writes me a check for the deposit, pretending to not remember what the figure was, and gives me fifty dollars over the original sum. I walk back down to the bus office and wait. The clouds begin to roll in. I think of the girl, the girl, especially, yes. The bus is late and I almost hope it doesn't show. The rain starts down and the bus pulls in. I climb aboard and stuff my purple bag into the overhead rack.

There are only six other passengers. The bus rumbles and squeaks and pulls out onto the highway. Most of the time when I leave a place it is a relief, even knowing I will never come back, I'm eager to get on. But this time it is different. I look out the scratched silver-blue window and watch Decorah fall away in the rain.

A Piano Player Enters the Room

for Dave Reutter

CHICK CHOM TANG AND I ARE VERY MUCH ALIKE: CHILDLESS, suburban-bred, TV-culture baby boomers who somehow missed the boat on the Promises of Youth. Neither of us has ever come close to marriage. Both of us have been poor (by American standards) all of our adult lives. As solid and supportive as our families have been, they probably still regard us as disappointments, difficult to explain in the annual Christmas letter, the funny uncles in the family tree. We console each other in weekly beer-drinking sessions, telling fond tales of childhood and ancient female conquest. The strong difference between us is that, while I try to be realistic about my circumstances, Chick believes his life has not yet begun.

Chick has been my next-door neighbor at this small-town residential motel in central Kansas for almost two years. Tall and pale, with long dangling arms and tousled brown hair and a large purplish nose, Chick was born in Topeka, Kansas, and raised in Greensboro, North Carolina. His real name is Melvin Bodger Witherby. He calls himself Chick because he dislikes the name Melvin. The Chom Tang part came to him, he claims, with mystical and artistic insinuations, while he was walking the streets of Honolulu at age twenty-eight as a first-year member of the United States Navy.

Chick's favorite subjects are Tarzan, Carlos Castaneda, L. Ron Hubbard (the science-fiction writer who founded Scientology), music, and especially art. Though primarily a piano player, Chick has also mastered many other instruments, including the banjo, the violin, and the tenor saxophone. He admits that he doesn't quite have the talent to be a Charlie Parker or a Thelonious Monk, and over the years he has lost much of his interest in playing. 'Music is my rudder,' he likes to say. 'It has brought me this far, but it is behind me now.'

Chick is forty-one (I am forty-three) and attends the state university two miles east of here. He entered on a music scholarship and six months later switched to physics. Now he is an art major. That he has not become a successful artist, painter, writer, or musician, he insists, is the fault of his parents, who did not give him proper and, more important, early enough exposure in these areas. He has given up on his parents, his brothers and sisters too. They don't understand or appreciate him or what he is trying to become. They can't relate to Chick Chom Tang. He has no more contact with his friends back in North Carolina either. He subsists on and pays tuition with his G.I. Bill and government loans. Most of his life he has lived under the sponsorship or protection of some institution or relative. Chick was honorably discharged from the navy when he was thirty-five. He has not worked in two years and intends to keep it this way.

Chick likes to think that once his art studies are completed, he will become creative — not in any minor problem-solving or songwriting sense, as he is now, but in a manner that borders on, perhaps even falls within, the realm of genius. He believes, by the empirical application of certain as-yet-unknown principles, the mysteries of the creative mind will someday be revealed to him. He has read numerous books on the subject and reconstructed the creative process of many famous artists. He is working on a brain-hemisphere theory, a return-to-the-cradle theory, and a psychological system of creativity induction called 'flux' that will take ten or fifteen years to master. Once he has assimilated and harmonized all of these, he believes, he will be privileged with artistic knowledge beyond that of any other practitioner on earth.

Beginning at age forty-six, Chick asserts, he will find his ideal mate, sire children, and teach them all the valuable things his parents never taught him: how to tend animals, fix cars, defend themselves, create art, and so forth. He will not likely produce symphonies and sculpture until much later. A grand future must be meticulously prepared for. All great ideas must be thoroughly explored: love, for example, which

Chick insists is a force, not an emotion. I believe he says this because he does not understand or is too afraid of love, the emotion, and quantifying it as if it were a physical property takes the sting out of not having been successful at it. This is also, I'm sure, what he is trying to do with art, perhaps with every intangible goal he finds unobtainable in life.

Chick explains to me that the reason I have failed in all my relationships with women is because I don't understand this elemental principle of *love = force*. (I thought it was because I was a chump.) This doesn't explain why he, too, has failed in all his relationships, but that is another matter. Chick is presently infatuated with a fellow art student who is twenty-one. His feelings for her are clearly unreciprocated, and I have tried to convince him of this. I don't often directly challenge Chick's fantasies, but it's only right to tackle a blind man about to be run over by a streetcar: he already has two formal sexual-harassment charges (trumped up, he says) filed against him at the university. One more and he will be out on his own, with no place to turn. He has run out of friends, relatives, and institutions. I try to jar him with the facts: 'Look at yourself, Chick. You're forty-one. You've never had any kind of lasting relationship with a woman. Do you think things are suddenly going to change? Why would they?'

For our weekly beer-drinking sessions, Chick and I always convene in my room (with the blue vinyl armchair, the shamrock green carpet, the cracked vanity mirror, and the chintzy Second

Empire desk and dresser). He is not equipped for visitors. Chick is a self-proclaimed misanthrope and anarchist. I am the only person in this complex he can stand, the only one who can relate to him, the only one patient and interested enough to pursue his company. He enjoys talking about himself. Our discussions are sometimes reminiscent of a clinical counseling session, with me in the role of counselor.

'Have you ever prayed to God to die?' he asks.

'Oh, yes. One or two hundred times.'

He holds out his hands. 'And here we are.'

'God doesn't want us to die, I guess.'

'Maybe he isn't there to answer our prayers.'

'Maybe asking God to die isn't really a prayer.'

'He only kills the weak ones.'

'Then he should've killed me years ago.'

Chick smiles at me with pity. He often boasts that he is descended from Viking stock. 'What is my weakness?' he asks.

'I don't want to recite your weaknesses,' I say, 'because I don't like people reciting mine. I know what mine are. You know what yours are.'

'C'mon,' he urges. 'Tell me what my weakness is.'

I try to think of a friendly way to say that he lives in a fantasy world. He believes, for instance, that he can intercept the thoughts and feelings of women who are in love with him. He consults with and receives messages from The Universe. He believes that he possesses telepathic powers that allow him to communicate with plants and insects. At twenty-six, he lived in a small converted garage with a roach problem, which he claims he solved one night after speaking telepathically with a female albino roach 'emissary' who appeared out of the drain in his bathroom sink. He once lived for free on a little plot of wooded land in North Carolina, where he walked about naked and climbed trees for a few months. Trees, he claims, are his only source of love. He planted tomatoes too late this year, but talked with confidence of their extraordinary ability to last and even produce through the winter. (His only knowledge of plants comes from a book called *The Findhorn Garden*, a modern account of a miraculous Scottish garden invested with pagan spirits.) Chick conversed with his tomatoes daily and the tomatoes instructed him in what to do: which weeds to pull, when to water, and so on. When harvest time came, his tomatoes were rather small and sickly, many of them splitting and decomposing on the vine before they could ripen. All the plants died with the first frost in late October, and they now hang brown against their string restraints, the green fruit rotting into the ground. Chick believes that the concept of destruction is a flaw in the universal plan. When I admitted to him that I often had to write ten bad stories to get a single good one, he refused to believe me. Only later did he identify some defect as the source of my difficulty.

So now, when he asks me to name his weakness, I summarize his general outlook on life by saying, I hope kindly: 'You're too idealistic.'

'Wrong,' he says, with a hearty, easy grin. 'I'm lazy.'

CHICK'S MOST RECENT FANTASY CONSTRUCTION — THE imminent discovery of the origin of creativity — appears to have been influenced by my rather late and mild success as a writer, which has taken the form of a few fan letters, one visit from three admiring strangers, and invitations from a coffeehouse for a reading and an alternative newspaper for an interview. Most impressive to Chick is the money, my sudden ability to buy expensive beer and take a trip home to visit my parents: all this just for sitting in my little room and making things up in front of a computer. (And I've only been at it for twenty years!) To Chick, this seems like a good gig. If art can exonerate an undistinguished, middle-aged, motel-dwelling loner like me, why couldn't it do the same for him?

'I'm thinking of writing some stories,' he tells me.

'Oh, really? What for?'

'To make some money,' he says with a big smile.

Every time we get together, Chick and I spend at least an hour talking about creativity. He is determined to figure this thing out. I tell him in so many words that he won't.

'It's a gift,' I say. 'You either have it or you don't.'

'I don't believe in gifts,' he says. 'Mozart, Beethoven, Rembrandt—they were all exposed early to their craft. They all started young.'

'And you don't think they had gifts?' I say. 'Do you know how many people were exposed young to painting and piano playing who weren't geniuses? I started playing the violin when I was seven. I was terrible. I hated it. I had no gift.'

'You didn't have the right teacher.'

'That doesn't explain why one student becomes a great violinist and another doesn't.'

'It's learning,' Chick says. 'Learning and memory and exposure to certain ideas at the right age.'

I sense him fuming again at his parents for their lack of foresight in not preparing him to be a genius. I recite to him a few examples that contradict his theory: Raymond Chandler not beginning to write until the Great Depression ruined his future as an oil executive; Joseph Conrad not learning English, the language in which he composed his novels, until his mid-thirties; Carson McCullers moving to New York from small-town Georgia, intending to study music and turning to fiction only after losing all her money on the subway.

Chick insists that once a thing is learned, it can be repeated indefinitely.

'You're talking about formula, which doesn't apply to art,' I say. 'Harper Lee never wrote another novel after *To Kill a Mockingbird*. If she knew how to write one great novel, why didn't she do it again?'

'Maybe she didn't want to.'

'More likely, she had only one story to tell.'

'I don't agree with that,' he says. 'If she'd wanted to, she could've written another. Look at Steinbeck and his repeated use of the Knights of the Round Table.'

'That's theme.'

'But he uses it over and over, doesn't he?'

'Yes, he does.'

'Don't you see? That's an application of a known system.'

'If creativity is an application of a known system, why do good directors make so many bad films?'

Employing logic with Chick takes almost more energy than it's worth. But I take no satisfaction in simply humoring him all night, even if we are merely passing the time. Chick's belief in the eventual discovery of the principles of creativity is just that, belief, an article of faith. Like many people, he operates on the false premise that intelligence begets creativity, that because he possesses one he's entitled to the other. He assumes that since he understands art he should be able to produce art.

But smart does not translate into art. This is illustrated by the many dull celebrities who croon, paint, strum, draw, rap, act, and write brilliantly. Conversely, many bright people are left to consider or criticize or stand in line and pay money to admire the work of their intellectual inferiors. Creativity, like beauty or athleticism or a sense of humor, is simply the luck of the draw. Perhaps it will one day be traced genetically (along with beauty, athleticism, and a sense of humor). Then it will be duplicated in the laboratory, dissected and distilled by scientists, and distributed for consumption in the Perfect World Where Everyone Is Happy. But meanwhile, now, in the Land of Reality, it cannot be acquired.

Chick can't accept this, though, because it undermines the very foundation upon which his fragile notions and his grandiose future rest. The secret to a creative life (which promises vindication and escape from his ordinary existence) must be accessible to him somehow, just as one might sign up for a sky-diving class or obtain a real-estate license or learn how to juggle. He wants something easy and indoor and formulaic: $A + B = CREATIVITY$. If you're interested in becoming rich, I suggest you produce an infomercial guaranteeing to divulge the Ten Easy Steps to Creativity. Chick would buy your product, and so would a million others like him.

Chick is never shy about giving me advice, especially about my writing. He knows I am no genius. What genius would work all day in a radio-antenna factory to write stories at night and then discard ninety percent of them? He is particularly appalled by the abysmal success-to-failure ratio, and by the fact that I have completed sixteen novels, not one of them marketable. 'You'll never learn how to write a novel if you don't master form,' he advises me sternly.

Since Chick doesn't write and doesn't even read fiction (except for Tarzan books and L. Ron Hubbard), I am somewhat amused by this. All of the examples from literature that he uses to make his points he has borrowed from me and reworked to fit his argument.

'How would I go about that?' I ask.

'Simple,' he says. 'You copy the masters.'

'In my business, we call that plagiarism.'

'Picasso copied the masters,' he says. 'Seurat, Cézanne.' He recites a long list of painters who became great by copying others and who continued to copy even at the height of their careers.

'Painting is different from writing,' I say.

'It all boils down to the same thing,' he insists. 'Composition, mood, value.'

'Except that language has to have specific meaning,' I say.

'Music and painting are languages too,' he counters.

'But the problems are different. One is literal, the others symbolic.'

'It's all symbolic,' he says emphatically.

'The word *novel* means "new",' I say. 'All good novels are new. I can't write "Variations on *Catcher in the Rye*" or "*Great Gatsby* in B Minor." A writing style is discovered or invented, not copied.'

'You're too left-brained,' he says.

'All right, I'm too left-brained.'

'If Picasso were here, he would tell you.'

'If Picasso were here, he wouldn't know what left-brained meant.'

Chick laughs nervously. Which means I have won the argument, though it makes no difference; the argument is irrelevant: either you produce something creative, or you don't.

FOR THANKSGIVING, CHICK HAS NOWHERE SPECIAL TO GO. He mentions an aunt in Abilene, but he has no desire to go where he will not be appreciated or understood. It was the same last Thanksgiving and I imagine it has been this way since he became Chick Chom Tang, the Don Quixote of Unrequited Genius. I suggest we roast a duck. He eagerly agrees. I tell him to bring the stuffing. This pleases him. I've worked in a lot of kitchens, so I usually do all the cooking—all the cleaning, as well. Chick simply lets me take care of him. That is the only arrangement he understands. 'I'll bring the wine too,' he says.

I roast a duck with apricot sauce, boil potatoes with onions and milk and chicken stock, then mash them, poach asparagus, and bake (thaw) a Mrs. Smith's Dutch apple pie. Chick brings oyster-spinach stuffing and a three-liter box of Franzia merlot.

'The stuffing isn't too good,' he says.

'Where did you get the recipe?'

'Off the Internet.'

'Did you follow the directions?'

'I changed a few things...' He sulks a little as we eat. His creativity has failed him again. 'Everything else is good,' he grumbles.

'Everything is good,' I say.

When we've finished dinner, I clear the table. Chick tips back in his chair and watches me, sipping from his jar of wine and tapping his big foot to the cool jazz of Chet Baker. He tells me that Chet Baker was a lifelong junkie, says that it's hard to find a good cool-jazz musician who wasn't a junkie. He makes heroin sound like a source of creativity: stick a needle in your arm and push the plunger down on a syringe full of cool jazz. We drink the wine and get slightly drunk. The sun goes down. It is a warm evening in Kansas. Chick excitedly expresses a new idea about creativity, a variation on his brain-hemisphere theory: he is going to start painting with both hands. I tell him about Yeats's left-handed automatic writing, Kesey writing *Cuckoo's Nest* on LSD, Coleridge composing on opium, Bukowski's drunk-trance states. Chick is pleased and comforted by gimmicks. I feel as if I am misleading him, filling his syringe with cool jazz.

At the end of the evening, the conversation turns to religion. Chick has an astounding belief system, a combination of Tarzan, Scientology, Carlos Castaneda, Darwinism, and nature worship, interspersed with convenient bits of the larger, more traditional disciplines, especially the Eastern methodologies. He defends his makeshift faith stoutly, believing his organization of thought infallible. Since I've known him, he has been trying to enlighten me, teach me, help me see the way, stubborn and thick-witted as I am. To his dismay, I have managed instead to erode and even dissolve many of his positions. Lately he has been concentrating on his version of apocalypse, which will occur in forty years and involves a natural revolution, green versus evil, wherein the earth will revert to a state of unblemished wilderness rivaling or exceeding the Garden before the appearance of Adam and Eve.

'How?' I say incredulously. 'You've got six billion people flushing their toilets every twenty minutes.'

'It'll happen,' he says. 'You'll see.'

'You don't even recycle your beer cans, Chick.'

'It won't matter,' he says.

'Nothing on earth is going to change,' I say. 'It's been the same place for 4.8 billion years. It's a design. It's this way for a reason.'

He manages to light a cigarette without breaking eye contact. He seems to think that eye contact will help him win the argument. Perhaps he is sending telepathic signals to my subconscious. 'You watch,' he says with a shake of his finger as he finishes his jar of wine.

I consider reminding him that in forty years we will both very likely be dead—then I realize that he is probably referring in some way to this event, his own death, and the promise of paradise to follow, though I don't believe he understands this himself.

What I don't realize is that I have struck a blow deep into the heart of Chick's fantasy life, his only life. I have good intentions, though. My rounding up his vagaries and wayward ideas one by one and examining them comes out of a love of truth and order, not cruelty. I hope to see him someday get a job, have a girlfriend or even a wife, maybe return to his family, or at least have one sustained friendship outside of mine. But Chick doesn't see it this way. And it won't be long before my subtle and systematic assault on his dream world will cause him to angrily declare our friendship is over.

I think about Chick and how, throughout his life, he has always managed to falter just at the point where he might succeed. The purpose of this pattern seems clear to me. Call it fear of failure or fear of success; I don't see much difference.

He would succeed, but he knows that a minor success would fall miserably short of his fantastic expectations. It would be the same as failure. Hence his constant changes in course and location, his withdrawal from the hopeless and difficult reality of labor and social interaction, his defiant declaration of anarchism and misanthropy, his construction of an unassailable imaginary fortress called the future.

'What do you think about this?' I say, and I begin reading to him from a book called *The Religion of Spirit*, by an obscure nineteenth-century Jewish philosopher named Solomon Formstecher, who said that there were only two basic religions: the religion of nature (paganism) and the religion of spirit (ethics).

Chick listens for a while, then bristles. 'Why are you reading this to me?'

'Because we were talking about religion.'

'Well, it's a bunch of malarkey,' he says. Chick regards most of my religious positions and arguments as heresy.

'It's just an opinion,' I say. 'You can take it or leave it.'

'You're a fool,' he says.

'Why, because I read obscure nineteenth-century idealist philosophy?'

'No, because you think you know so much.'

'I don't know a thing, Chick. We're just passing the time.'

'You watch,' he says. 'In forty years it will happen.'

I'm not going to argue with him anymore. 'Maybe it will,' I say.

Chick seems satisfied.

Bingo Clock

HIRAM AND I ARE SITTING IN A LITTLE TEN-STOOL REDNECK bar called Betty's on Ouachita Avenue in Hot Springs, Arkansas. We've worked together for three months as dinner cooks at the Arlington Hotel, but tonight is his last night—he's leaving for Oklahoma in the morning and I am seeing him off. A Mariners-Yankees game is playing up in the corner on ESPN. Seattle is ahead five to nothing. The barmaid has turned the jukebox off, but some crazy old guy is still out on the floor waltzing by himself.

Hiram has already drunk a six-pack. He drains his seventh can and bangs the empty on the bar. 'I sure as hell won't miss that chef,' he says.

'You never did like him much.'

'No,' he says. 'I never did. And I won't miss that damn rathole of a hotel either. I never worked in such a lousy place.'

I've worked in lousier places, but I agree with him.

'I won't miss Arkansas either.'

'You're in a hell of a mood.'

He yanks a wad of bills out from his front pocket and waves at the girl for two more, dribbling ashes from the perennial cigarette hanging from his lips. He's been buying all the beer tonight and I haven't yet figured out why.

Hiram Jones is fifty-two, a full-blooded Seneca-Cayuga Indian, though with light skin, calm gray eyes, and short, steel-colored hair neatly parted on the right with a little dab of Brylcreem, he looks more like a Republican. Hiram grew up in the same part of Oklahoma as his hero, Mickey Mantle. His favorite Mickey Mantle story is the sandlot tale about how Mickey hit one over the river. Nobody'd ever done that before, nobody's done it since. Hiram played professional ball himself for the AAA St. Louis Cardinals affiliate. He says he had a shot at the majors, but wrecked his arm in Vietnam.

He crushes out his cigarette and lights another, glancing up wistfully at the television. The Yanks have scored five runs on two hits in the bottom of the sixth to tie the game. Hiram clanks beer number eight on the bar and raises his hand for two more. I am a full three behind him, letting my untouched cans pile up along the napkin dispenser. Usually we take turns buying and I can pace him a little, but there's no slowing him down tonight.

'You can't trust anyone anymore,' he growls. 'Not one damn person, not even your own wife.'

His wife is white. I met her once when she came to visit him in the hospital and she seemed nice enough, the Mamie Eisenhower type. Supposedly she sent him here to Arkansas three months ago to test out retirement possibilities, though they already own a nice retirement home on a lake in Oklahoma. The circumstances remain a mystery to me. All I know is that he is bitter about her and holds her accountable for something, perhaps the incredible streak of bad luck that has plagued him since he landed, starting the first week when he cut himself twice, once with a boning knife, once with an ice chisel — both hospital trips. In the next few weeks his grandson became ill with some incurable disease, his pregnant daughter was diagnosed with terminal cancer and lost the child, his drunken son got in a wreck, killing a sixteen-year-old girl and gravely injuring another (the last I heard manslaughter charges were still pending). Two weeks later Hiram began passing kidney stones. He was in the hospital for two days and missed a week of work.

'When I get back home,' he says, 'I'm going to fill a cooler with beer and go out on the pier and fish all night for catfish, fish till the sun comes up. That's what I miss more than anything,' he says. 'Fishing.'

'Sounds good,' I say.

'I don't give a damn if I catch anything or not,' he says. 'I just like being alone.'

'I hear that.'

He raises his hand again. 'Give us a couple more down here, will you...'

The barmaid turns us out at midnight and we stumble up the street. I live about four blocks away in a small apartment above the Prince Electronics Building. Hiram lives only three blocks away in an upstairs sleeping room at the Bryant House. It is springtime, the smell of rain in the air, a lovely time of year in the South. The town, except for the private clubs, is rolled up tight.

'I don't feel like going home,' says Hiram. 'Let's get another beer.'

We wander up Ouachita through the old downtown section of Hot Springs. The crickets jingle and the frogs belch, and if you listen carefully you can even hear the teenagers mating up in the hills. We find a club called Acapulco's, a new place, and pay a dollar 'membership' apiece. A loud band is playing Creedence and Bad Company covers. Hiram turns straight for the bar and retrieves four cans of Coors. We migrate to a booth in back. I am relieved to see that Hiram has passed out of gloom and misery and entered the brotherly love stage. He drains his fifteenth can and shouts over the music what a wonderful guy I am.

Hiram has cooked all his life, mostly in Oklahoma. He started out as a teenager frying burgers in some drive-in snack bar in the 1950s and never stopped. I've cooked most of my life too, but I wasn't even born when Hiram was working that snack bar. Hiram doesn't act, dress, or look Indian, and he doesn't talk about it either. He's just a regular guy who works hard when it's busy, smokes cigarettes over by the steamer when it's slow, loses a little money here and there betting football games, tells jokes that aren't too funny, and likes to have a few beers at Betty's after work. In the three months I've known him he's brought up the subject of Indians exactly once, and that was simply to tell me where he was from. But aliens are experimenting on him or a nefarious bartender has slipped Dr. Jekyll Drops into his sixteenth beer because now, out of the blue, he's begun to rave about Indians. His face has changed too, a hard polished red mask with a sharp hawk's nose curving out of it, the corners of his narrowed eyes pinched with anger. 'Oklahoma,' I hear him growling, 'is nothing but a government cattle pen for Indians.'

I don't know what to say. I feel as if I've just walked into the room. I blubber something about having Indian blood myself.

'You're a white man,' he sneers.

I stare at him for a minute, leaning back in the booth. 'All right, Hiram,' I say, finally. 'I'm a white man, but I'm a man. And so are you. And that's all that matters.'

'I'm an Indian,' he gruffs.

I feel my head lunging forward. 'An Indian first and a man second?'

'Yes.'

'Why?'

'Because that's my heritage.'

'What's heritage?' I flop my hand around in the air. 'You're Hiram Jones. American. Free man. You can go where you like. Work where you like...'

Hiram says, 'My father taught me that the white man is better than the Indian.'

'Your father was from a different time.'

'It doesn't change anything,' he says.

'You still believe this?'

'Yes.'

'Why?'

He shakes his head, puffing stubbornly on his cigarette. His eyes are moist and the corners of his mouth are twisted haughtily down. The look says: *you will never understand*.

'Explain it to me, Hiram,' I insist. 'I'd really like to know how white people are better than Indians.'

He sizzles down his beer and slams the empty on the table. 'Indians are no good,' he says.

I derail the conversation. He is beginning to look belligerent. 'How much does it cost to join that cook's union in Vegas?' I ask him. Hiram worked at Caesar's Palace for about ten years, broiled a million steaks, even saw Frank Sinatra one night (who owned half of Caesar's at the time) strolling majestically through the kitchen. He liked Vegas, would've stayed if he hadn't had kids. I've been thinking about going there myself. Even non-union cooks make seventy-five a shift, right off the bus.

Hiram nods at me. He knows what I'm trying to do but answers my question anyway. 'Couple hundred bucks,' he grunts. Then he stands up and shuffles off to the bathroom. When he returns a few minutes later he has a Coors in each hand and a smirk on his face. He sits down, slides me over a beer, and says, 'I want you to have something of mine before I go.'

I take a sip from my beer. 'What is it?'

'It's a clock.'

'What do I want with a clock?'

'It's a silent clock,' he says, his face shining with a wild leer that I don't like at all. 'Keeps real good time.'

'That's nice,' I say, 'but I've already got a clock.'

'It's a small clock.'

I take a long drink from my beer.

'You don't want the clock?' he says.

'Not unless you really want me to have the clock, Hiram.'

He peers at me for a good minute, a funny half-drunk simper crawling over his face as if he's about ready to burst out laughing. Then he takes a couple of quick swigs from his can. 'I wouldn't want you to have that clock anyway.'

'OK,' I say.

He swings back around to the earlier subject, the general worthlessness and inferiority of Indians. He rants for a while longer about his tribe, telling me they are a bunch of drunkards and thieves, etc. Uncle Sam has bought the last of their pride, etc. I stop trying to respond, only do my imitation of a store mannequin drinking Coors. Eventually he works around to the story of how his tribe built a bingo hall. He recounts to me in detail how the bingo hall went broke. 'It's an empty building now,' he tells me. 'Boarded up. They sit on the front steps and drink whiskey. It never made a dime.'

I scratch my jaw and nod at him.

Then he says, 'You remind me of my wife.'

'Hardly any way to construe that as a compliment, Hiram,' I say.

'She's a good Christian woman,' he says.

'Wave a napkin at me or something when you're ready to make sense.'

He sneers: 'You're always talking about increasing the amount of faith and goodness in the world. That's how she talks…'

'I am not *always* talking about increasing the amount of faith and goodness in the world, Hiram. Besides, you're the one buying all the beer.'

He stares at me wordlessly for a few moments, then lowers his gaze. His tone is dejected. 'My wife bought me a souvenir clock from that bingo hall.'

'She what?'

'She gave it to me before I left Oklahoma.'

'Was that her idea of a joke?'

He shrugs and looks desolately away. 'I don't know.'

'Doesn't she know how you feel?'

'Yes,' he says, his voice cracking. 'She does.'

Then he says that he thinks that the clock is the source of all his problems, the kidney stones, the loss of his cancer-stricken daughter's child, the manslaughter charges pending against his son, the injuries at work. As he talks he grows more adamant about the clock. It is an evil clock, a symbol of the downfall of his tribe. A curse.

'And you wanted to give me the thing?' I say.

'I was only playing with you,' he says, with a nervous flash of teeth. 'I only wanted to see what you would say.'

Now I know why he has bought all the beer. Softening me up, trying to palm a hex off on me. Not that I believe in hexes, but it's the thought that counts. To cover my disappointment in him I walk to the bar for a round, the first I've bought all night. He is in near despair when I return. 'I hate that fucking clock,' he says.

'Why don't you get rid of it?'

'I can't.'

'Why not?'

'I don't know,' he says, wiping at his eyes. He is so distraught he looks insane, groping at his scalp, mussing up his gleamy Brylcreemed hair. 'I've tried to break it but it won't break.' He looks up at me forlornly. 'You don't believe me, do you?'

'If you believe it that's all that matters.'

'I know it sounds crazy,' he says, 'but I know it's that fucking clock.'

I lean back in the booth. This is my first authentic brush with Evil Spirit Investing Inanimate Object, which I am only familiar with through old Twilight Zone episodes. I look around the room. Without my noticing, the band has quit, packed up, and left. 'Club members' are beginning to file out, though no one has yet spoken those dreaded words 'last call.' The prospect of the evil bingo clock not only stirs my interest, but seems to have sobered me up slightly. I rise and stroll to the bar and order two more. Hiram informs me when I return that he has decided he is going to give the clock away.

'To me, right?'

'No,' he says. 'I was just kidding.'

'Right.'

'I think I'll give it to the chef,' he says.

Diabolical laughter comes bubbling out of my throat.

'I can't do it, though,' he says.

'No,' I agree. 'You couldn't give it to your worst enemy.'

'How am I going to get rid of it then?'

I think for a minute. This is a funny problem. I don't believe in voodoo, in ghosts, in astrology, in evil clocks, but I do believe in this man across from me in agony. 'Well,' I say. 'You can't destroy evil, can't burn it, can't take it apart, can't throw it away, not when it's been assigned to you...' I check his face. He is listening carefully. 'I guess the only solution is to transfer ownership.'

'I'll give it to the chef,' he says.

We both laugh again.

I twirl and finish my beer. 'Let's go have a look at that clock. I'm anxious to see what it looks like.'

'You're going to be disappointed,' he says. 'It's just a shitty little souvenir clock.'

'That's how evil works,' I explain, now comfortable in my new role as demonological expert. 'It always occupies the most unassuming forms. The guy who goes on the murdering spree is always the mildest one in the neighborhood. The neighbors never have a clue...'

'Yeah,' he says.

'Don't worry, Hiram,' I say, patting him on the back. 'We're going to get rid of that clock tonight, somehow, I promise.'

Rain is falling softly outside; the streets are wet and steaming; the raindrops, lit by streetlight, race like little glass beads down the telephone wires and plop with a wooden rattle into the waxy leaves of the magnolia trees. We walk briskly through the rain and in three minutes we are standing damply in his room at the Bryant House and I am holding the infamous clock, a sad little gold-faced digital timepiece, one of those disposable plastic gizmos you stick on your dashboard, except it is embedded in a hard plastic L-shaped pedestal with the name of the tribe and the bingo hall stamped in chintzy gold on the front of it.

'I just want to stomp on it,' says Hiram.

'Looks pretty tough,' I say, turning it over in my hands.

'It is,' he says. 'My wife said you could break it if you fooled with those things on the back.'

'It wouldn't break, though, huh?'

'No.'

I start fooling around with the things on the back and only manage to screw up the date and time. Hiram has another clock on the dresser, a loud-ticking, old-fashioned, red fire-truck clock with big gold bells on it, the exact opposite of the evil bingo clock. The fire-truck clock reads three thirty. I try to restore the correct time on the evil clock (discounting all the superstitious notions fluttering into my head), but finally give up and stuff it into my jacket pocket. 'Let's go get some breakfast,' I say. 'I'll drive.'

HIRAM'S OLD 1976 IMPALA SITS UNDER A MOUND OF magnolia leaves that look as if they've been heaped on with a pitchfork. I climb inside the driver's side and immediately sink about a foot through decaying foam rubber and collapsed springs. The floor offers up the dank leafy odor of an old log cabin abandoned in the forest. It takes me a few minutes to start the car—the battery is nearly dead—and now I can't get it into gear.

'We have to wait a few minutes for it to warm,' Hiram explains.

But after a few minutes the transmission still won't engage. Finally Hiram comes around, I slide over, and he begins gunning the engine and jimmying the shifter; he revs the car to screaming, clunking the shifter. I wait for a rod to come flying through the hood. Suddenly the windshield wipers jump on, slapping away a stack of leaves, and we leap off the curb out of the mountain of magnolia leaves and zigzag out into the street.

Hiram isn't even close to being qualified to drive. He misses a couple of turns, sprawls across the white lines, takes corners as if he's piloting the *Exxon Valdez*. There isn't a soul out but wouldn't it be fitting if Hiram got pulled over and hauled off to jail, I think, just one more piece of bad luck.

'How do you feel with that clock?' he says.

'It feels kind of hot,' I admit. 'But I'm not worried about it.' I tell him I have some spiritual power, which is partly beer, partly bluff, the rest not believing in spirits in the first place. But the main point, I emphasize, is that it isn't my clock.

'Yeah,' he replies dryly, peering up through the steering wheel at the empty street weaving gently before us in the rain.

'I just hope we make it to the Waffle House, Hiram.'

'I do too,' he says earnestly. 'Who are we going to give that clock to?'

'Nobody,' I say. 'We're just going to get some breakfast.'

'Boy, am I hungry,' he says. He nudges the medium, then overcorrects and almost hits the curb on the other side.

'Pay attention to the road.'

'Who're we going to give it to then?'

'We're just going to leave it on the counter,' I say. 'We'll let it find someone.'

'But that's not fair...is it?'

'What do you call it when people take things that don't belong to them?'

'Stealing?'

'And what do they deserve?'

'I don't know.'

'Look, once they figure out the clock's a curse they can do the same thing we did. That's the way it works, Hiram, the chain of destiny.'

'What if they get killed or something?'

'They don't have to take the clock, Hiram. Besides, it

might only be bad luck to you. To someone else it could just be a clock.'

He turns left into the Waffle House parking lot. The diner is packed. The rain has finally stopped. Hiram has to make about eight passes before he finally gets the car parked straight.

We sit at the counter and I set the clock down in front of us. No one notices. Why should they? The waitress peers down at us with a mixture of weariness and bland amusement. Two more drunks finishing the night up with pork and fried eggs, and they've brought their clock along with them. For some reason, I hope she isn't the one who ends up with the clock.

I've never had a bad breakfast at the Waffle House, and I'm so hungry I order another. The plan has finally sifted into Hiram's skull and he can see that it is going to work. Whoever takes the clock deserves what they get. Hiram is suddenly laughing at everything, his old self, a joy to be around. Not once does he glance at the clock in front of us at a slight angle snicking away the wrong time, stubbornly blinking the wrong date. We take our time, have another cup of coffee, then pay the bill at the register by the door. I roll a toothpick out of the dispenser and we stroll out into the fresh, cool, rain-scrubbed air.

How I Lost My Mind and Other Adventures

for Sara Sherman

I TOOK THE BUS FROM IOWA DOWN TO MEMPHIS, A FUNNY pressure in my chest, a nervous futility, an unaccountable fatigue. I walked along the railroad tracks and the streets of white clapboard houses, the air smelling of soap and tar. I passed a place called Duno's Lounge. There was a *Help Wanted* sign in the window but I couldn't go in. This had never happened to me before. I told myself I was just fed up with asking for minimum-wage jobs, that I needed a rest. I got a motel room along the creosote-smelling Wolf River and walked until I came to a market called Louie and Wu's on Warford Avenue, where I bought a can of Spaghetti-O's and two bananas and a box of week-old doughnuts on sale for ninety-nine cents.

I rode the bus from Memphis to Jackson, Mississippi, and walked the streets. I bought a paper and took it to a McDonald's, where I ate three cheeseburgers with a cup of coffee. I saw a job in the classifieds. With the wind blowing and rain threatening, I made phone calls, trying to find a room. No room, no job. Feeling oddly relieved, I walked to the Eudora Welty Library, where I visited 'The Writer's Room,' a glass-encased shrine filled with photos and memorabilia of the famous Mississippi authors: Welty and Faulkner and Thomas 'Tennessee' Williams. I studied a map, then went back to the bus depot and ate a candy bar and waited.

Laurel, Mississippi, was about the right size, the right look. There would be no excuses here. I simply had to find a job. I thought I might have Epstein-Barr virus, though I didn't even know what Epstein-Barr virus was. All I knew was that it made you tired, and that it lasted a long time. I walked down to the Safeway and bought a pound cake and oranges. Then I went back to my motel room and slept for two days.

The bus wound south through the worn-out Coca-Cola towns, the rain like smoke, the weeds growing up through the porches. In every park, plaza, or town square sat a war memorial. The graveyards with their fog-stained markers always had fresh flowers on the graves.

I was down to about seven hundred dollars when I met a guy on the bus who said there were oil-derrick jobs in

Houma, Louisiana, down on the delta: fourteen days on, seven days off; good money. I could make a few thousand in a few months, not have to work the rest of the year, find a nice place somewhere and sleep. He wrote down two addresses for me.

Houma was bigger than I had expected, a whole city built on two hundred millennia of collected river mud and items flushed from toilets as far away as Brainerd, Minnesota. I tried to walk to one of the addresses the guy had given me, but it turned out to be more than five miles from my motel, so I gave up.

I spent the next night in the New Orleans bus terminal. Behind me a kid played the world's loudest pinball machine. From outside someone threw a beer bottle at the window and it bounced off and shattered on the ground. I tried to call some friends on the pay phone, but no one was home. For the first time in my life, I wondered where I would go next.

If I'd had the money, I would've kept traveling forever. I liked sitting on a bus, looking down through the scratched blue windows. But at the rate I was going, I had about a month before my feet would be sticking out of a bunk at the Baptist Mission. I went to Hot Springs, Arkansas, where I had lived four years before, and stayed at the Holiday Motel on Ouachita Avenue for eighty-five dollars a week. I didn't even look to see how much money I had left. It was a nice little room with a ceiling fan. The oven in the kitchenette was broken. I boiled chicken potpies and drank iced water and lay under the slow-turning fan.

I think some part of me understood that I was about to lose my mind, even though, as far as I could see, there was no reason for me to lose my mind. Nothing like that had ever happened to me before. No family history of lunacy. I was young and strong. I was simply traveling around, trying to find a spot. I would get a job, stay as long as I liked, then move on. It was a romantic life, at least on paper. I'd been doing it for fifteen years.

But even the part of me that didn't realize I was about to lose my mind could see that something was wrong: the traveling had lost its meaning, and I couldn't see a place in the distance where it would ever end. I was writing stories and poems, but having no success. I had given up, for the time being, any idea of finding a woman. The thought of starting over again from scratch in a new town — the strangers, the empty room, the low-paying job where they would lead me through the door marked *Hazardous Chemicals*, the willful isolation and poverty — seemed like self-flagellation. I had a cough like a flock of wild Canadian geese. I had far less than the amount of money it would take to make a reasonable stand. Every place was wrong before I even got off the bus. I physically could not ask someone to lead me through the door marked *Hazardous Chemicals*. I would not have put it this way at the time, but I needed help. An institution was the natural choice. Voluntary commitment. The name of the institution I had in mind was Iowa State University.

I took a slow bus back to Iowa, my last state of legal residence, my anxiety now converted to a sluggish and complacent sense of defeat. It was late spring. I had enough money for two weeks at the Ames Motor Lodge, at $125 a week. I got a job at a transmission factory. On my first day, they led me through the door marked *Hazardous Chemicals*, and for the next two weeks I sprayed, cleaned, and painted until I graduated to the Hymco, a belt-driven cleaner like a dishwasher that steamed the grease off the newly machined parts. I wore goggles and earplugs. I ate lunch in the brightly lit lunch room with its walls of snack machines and bulletin boards filled with dazzling reminders and advice for idiots, and it was like being in elementary school all over again, right down to the steam-and-creamed-peas smell of it, and especially the gentle, switched-off eyes of my co-workers. It rained every day for three months. I walked two and a half miles to work in the cold rain and two and a half miles home in the hot rain. The town flooded that summer; it was the Great Flood of 1993.

I found a little basement apartment in the middle of town for $245 a month (it only flooded twice) and started college in the fall. I hadn't been in school for fifteen years. I got a federal loan and a Pell grant, quit the job at the transmission factory, and took a part-time janitorial position cleaning two restaurants and the city-hall gymnasium every weekend. I walked across the campus the first day of classes with all my books under my arm, and it was like being in a big amusement park: safe and clean, with plenty of trash cans and soda-pop machines and people in brown uniforms cleaning up after me. Everyone was happy. Even I was happy. As I walked along under the trees with the chattering, excited children, I wanted to laugh: I had voluntarily committed myself to the state institution.

Since I had a bunch of psychology credits saved up from my long-ago college experience, I decided to become a psychology major. I would be a drug counselor. It seemed the only thing I was really qualified to do, having spent ten years screwed up on drugs. Now that I was done with them, I felt I could help others with the knowledge I'd gained through my stupidity. But psychology was difficult to swallow. It was entirely theoretical. If you were good with words, you could become famous by making up your own psychological disorder: *Attention Deficit Disorder, Repressed Memory Syndrome, Mississippi Small Town Traveling Syndrome*. In the hundred years since the birth of psychology, two million maladies have thus been named, and twice as many theories proposed, but no one has yet come up with a single scientific law, rule, or objective formula. A hundred years is a long time to study something supposedly scientific without establishing even one empirical law.

In my spare time I wrote stories and sent them out. Although I had given up thinking it would happen, I began placing a story or a poem about once a month. They were little magazines that paid in copies. Nobody read them. Still, for a few days after each acceptance, I felt vaguely worthwhile.

I fell in love with my Spanish professor, though I had no intention of falling in love with anyone. Love is insanity, love is heroin, love is chocolate and brandy on fire blistering your lips and nose for the pleasure of your tongue. She was twenty-four, fresh from Spain, and spoke hardly any English. I spoke some Spanish, most of which I'd picked up working in kitchens. For the first few weeks of class, I served as translator for the Iowa children who knew only '*taco*' and '*hasta la vista*, baby.' She took me aside and thanked me. She was so short I wanted to kiss the top of her head. She smelled like a puppy. I wrote notes to her in Spanish on my class assignments; she wrote back in English. I thought to myself, *Finally, after all the hard lean years, something is coming my way.*

A story I sold for twenty-five dollars to a little San Francisco literary journal made a few ripples: it was nominated for a prize and inclusion in an anthology. Two strangers sent me letters of appreciation. I read the story one night at an open mike sponsored by the university creative-writing department. A low buzz of approval built as I read. A few people came over to my table afterward. An English professor began to seek me out. A high-school girl started coming over to my apartment. Someone asked me to read at the bookstore. For about a month, I was the greatest writer who ever lived.

Meanwhile, I was embarrassed to tell people my major. The more I studied psychology, the less sense it made. The professors seemed to be making it up as they went along, and were mostly goofy or creepy, which is what happens when you make things up all day and then try to live by

them. I discovered that, before I could be licensed by the
state to help drug addicts, I would have to get a master's
degree. I figured by the time I finished graduate school I
wouldn't be of much use to anyone. Besides, how could I
represent ideas I didn't believe in? I was like an atheist
studying to be a priest. Quitting school seemed the most
honorable thing to do, but I couldn't face going out again
on my own where they would make me mop floors and
cook hamburgers and spray for roaches, where I would live
around poor people who coughed and drank too much. I
was already a writer (even if I couldn't make a nickel at it),
so I decided to switch my major to English.

I had promised myself I would never deliberately enter an
English department or a writing program. Groups do not
create. 'Fainthearted animals move about in herds,' the poet
Alfred de Vigny wrote. 'The lion walks alone in the desert. Let
the poet always walk thus.' But I thought, *Well, I can get a job
teaching.* It wasn't quite selling out. I had lived in the real world.
I had done my time. Let someone else push the wheelbarrow
up the ramp for a while. I deserved these ivied walls, this
Pepsi-belching, government-subsidized comfort.

Many a morning that winter, I woke up in love and
walked three miles through the snow to school. I wrote
letters to my Spanish professor, stopped by her office, wooed
her. I was dazed by love, like someone hit in the forehead
with a two-by-four. She was too young. We had little in
common. I had no money and — though I didn't know it at
the time — no interest in settling down or becoming stable

in any fashion. At thirty-seven, I'd never had a relationship that worked. Nevertheless, I pursued her. She giggled and blushed and nodded, and we spoke crudely in each other's tongues. Her great appeal, I'm sure, was that we could not communicate.

I read whenever I could at the university open mike. People often came over to my basement apartment afterward—writers mostly, and writer-hopefuls, the English professor. The high-school girl came over late. She wanted me to bed her, but I wanted to be true to the Spanish professor, the real junkie-love of my life. I liked the high-school girl. She had spirit. She would be going off to Boston soon, to art school on a full scholarship. I worried that if she finished school she would have little chance of doing anything interesting: How can you expect to produce anything interesting or different while sitting in secure, climate-controlled comfort year after year, doing exactly what you're told? How do you get your certificate of long-standing conformity and then expect somehow to stand out from the crowd? I tried not to think of my own situation in the same light. I was the exception, which is what every member of the institution thinks. In any case, I had put too much into it to quit now. I was committed. I had a good chance at a ten-thousand-dollar writing fellowship, and would likely teach while attending graduate school. I couldn't imagine returning to a hot kitchen where stupid people turned hash browns on an eight-foot grill. I sat in the chilly, whirring, fluorescent-lit rooms and listened to the professors drone. Every evening, I switched on my computer and stared at the unfinished essays that were due on the eleventh or the twenty-third.

One day, an editor from New York wrote me. She'd seen one of my stories, she said, and thought it was 'beautiful.' She wondered if I could send her something for her new magazine. I told her I didn't have time to write anything for her new magazine. I was too busy writing an essay on Faulkner's mustache, and an essay on Beowulf's homosexual cousin Leonard, and an essay on Joyce Carol Oates' terrible childhood. I had to read six Victorian novels and eight African-American novels and two hundred other assorted literary chestnuts, warhorses, puzzle pieces, and party favors. But when I compared the things I was writing for my classes to the things I had written on a bus or in a Laundromat or in a room with only a desk and a bed and cockroaches doing water ballet across the walls and an old man coughing next door, it filled me with dread: I was going soft. The idea had been to get the psych degree, get back on my feet, and get out. Now I was dawdling in the English department, contemplating advanced degrees, and preparing to ask for another Pell grant. I'd already run out of money the semester before and taken out a provisional loan. Slowly, I'd become reliant on the U.S. government. I was even peevish when my checks were late: you don't want me to have to get a *job*, now do you? And I could see that even a master's degree wouldn't be enough: in order to ensure a lifetime of scholarly, mop-free leisure, I would have to get my doctorate at least, perhaps a post-doc. The days in which a college diploma alone offered admission into the educated noble class are gone. Anybody who can sign his name can get a student loan and an undergraduate degree. I was being driven, like every comfort-seeker, by the sheer volume of comfort-seekers.

About six weeks into my fourth term, I was sitting on a bench in the sunshine out in front of Ross Hall just before my literature-appreciation class, and I knew that if I spent another minute in one of those chilly, whirring, fluorescent-lit rooms or swallowed another ounce of the ignorance of the learned, I would be a certified sell-out, thirty thousand in debt, parroting the effeminate university line to keep my cozy vanilla-pudding job. If I didn't quit now (stop *lying* to yourself, man), there would be no turning back. I quit that day, that minute. As I passed through the dim, green, bureaucratic halls getting signatures and stamps of approval, the women staring into their computers couldn't understand why I was leaving. I was five thousand dollars in debt and only a semester away from graduating with honors, with a fellowship and teaching position awaiting me. 'Will you be attending part time?' the women asked. 'No.' 'Are you intending to return?' 'No.' It was like throwing a briefcase full of money off a bridge, or spending a year and a half working on an intricate toothpick sculpture, and then putting a match to it.

It took me a week to get a full-time job driving a truck—I needed to start paying off that debt. I began to work in earnest on the story for the editor in New York, and

I started a novel, an adaptation of the story that everyone had loved, English professors and high-school girls alike; the one nominated for a prize and inclusion in an anthology; the one oohed and aahed over at the open mike. I would merely expand it, add a theme.

It was the middle of winter. I drove my truck through the ice and snow every day. Twice, I went up to the Spanish professor's office in my trucker's clothes on my lunch break, but she wouldn't talk to me, wanted nothing to do with me: I had quit school and thrown away my future. She hadn't come all the way from Spain to date a college dropout. '*Soy un escritor,*' I told her: 'I am a *writer.*' But she did not understand. Or maybe it was me who did not understand: she was the fruit of the tree of knowledge, and I had left the garden to go dig ditches in Albuquerque. 'Have dinner with me,' I pleaded until she acquiesced. I waited at the restaurant, but she never showed. She was like the people who picked up your trash and filled the soda-pop machines and trimmed the trees: once you quit paying the money, they were gone. The amusement park was closed. The lights were off. I went home feeling as bad as I'd felt in a long time.

I drove the truck and worked on the novel and the story for the New York editor, staving off mental breakdown by staying busy every waking minute. In the evenings, the writers and writer-hopefuls and the high-school girl often came by. I was more interesting than ever now that I had thrown everything away. They were all eager to read the novel; they thought I must have something. I came home after delivering oxygen, acetylene, and propane and wrote for three hours. On the weekends I wrote all day. When I had saved seventeen hundred dollars and was six months ahead on my loan payments, I quit the job and wrote full time.

I finished the story at last and sent it off to New York. When the third draft of the novel was finished, I had three spiral-bound copies made and handed them out to my admirers. The responses seemed to take forever. Gradually, in kind and roundabout ways, the people who loved my writing told me that my brilliant book adapted from a prize-nominated story was an imitative, chicken-hearted, commercially motivated waste of time.

The story came back too. The editor didn't think she could use it in her magazine. She thanked me and asked if I could send something else. *Something else?* I thought. I worked on that story six months. It took me as long to write that story as it did to write the goddamn novel that wasn't any good either.

All right, I said to myself. I'll fix these things. I'll *make* them work. I've been at this game for quite a while, practicing, suffering, slaving, studying. I've sacrificed everything I have, done everything humanly possible. They *have* to work.

Sitting in front of the computer that night, working on the novel that really didn't stand a chance, trying to make it come together through sheer force of will, I finally had my nervous breakdown, mental collapse, whatever you want to call it. The pair of helpful, knitting hands that had been holding me up for so long stopped all at once, and the yarn fell to the floor. I felt myself sinking and breaking up, like a Chinese junk in a sea of green mud.

I remember walking the streets, bewildered terror, jewel-thin anguish, the cold, sinister clarity of sound. I wanted somebody to talk to, but there was no one. Besides, what would I say: 'I've lost my mind?' I talked to God instead. I said, 'Help me, God. Please, please, help me.' I couldn't seem to breathe. My guts clenched and churned like sweat shirts in an old Maytag. I was grinning up buckets of tears. The insides of my glasses were wet: my head would shrink up like an old pumpkin, then suddenly swell with a big spurt of boo-hoo-hoos, and the tears would fill my glasses.

I remember the grocery store. It looked too bright and fractured, tilting this way and that. I went in, seeing every-thing through the blurred prisms of dried salt on my glasses. I figured the employees would know at once I was insane. They would call the police, the hospital. I bought a pack of Old Golds. There was a yellow forty-cents-off coupon on the wrapper. The cashier peeled it off. I paid the money. I remember thinking, *I can be insane and still get forty cents off on a pack of Old Golds*.

I brought the cigarettes home and smoked them one after the other. I understood then why crazy people smoke cigarettes, why they consume them raggedly and unceasingly, leaving a fine blizzard of ashes wherever they go: there was something in nicotine like the gentle arms of an old killer; something in that marvelous poisonous plant alkaloid, evolved over millions of years for the purpose of deterring herbivores and insects, that was saving me. It was even better than college. Cheaper, too. I had a few more boo-hoo-hoos, and then I made a pact with those cigarettes. I said: 'You get me through the long days, and I'll let you kill me.'

That night, I started out of sleep with a piercing sadness, thinking of the Spanish professor I thought I loved. I had never been awakened by sadness before, by the face of a beautiful *española* whose irresistible mouth shaped the gorgeous chocolate syllables of failed romance. I got up and smoked a cigarette and sat in the dark. I stayed awake in the chair with my bare feet on the cold tile floor, the insanity-salve smoke spinning up in blue-gray spirals from between my fingers, the darkness filling up the curtains. I refused to return to bed. I did not want to be awakened by sadness again.

I have heard that God never puts more pressure on a man than he can bear, but that night I cracked from too much pressure. I don't blame God. God was saying, 'What are you doing? Where are your priorities? What kind of spineless little TV-believing materialist are you anyway? There is a room waiting for you at the end of the road: a table, light, time, a PaperMate Flexgrip Ultra Fine. Go to it. Stop making your life harder by trying to take the easy way out. There is no easy way out.' But I couldn't hear those words, couldn't hear God. I had to learn the lesson on my own.

The key to a long life is the perception of a long life, and no one perceives a longer life than one who cannot sleep. The clock might as well have been a painting of five minutes after three. For days I walked the streets or sat in a chair at the public library looking out the window. For the brief periods I was in my apartment, I smoked cigarettes with the windows open and the cold air rushing in. The walls buckled in on me; ghostly echoes spiraled down. I could not look at the novel. I did not want to wear the clothes or eat the food or sit in the furniture of the man who had done all those things that now made my hours intolerable.

I suddenly began to consider romance with a writer-hopeful who had come over to my apartment twice. She was not particularly attractive, but she was pleasant and intelligent. I thought — with whatever I was using for brains at the time — that I might marry her, even though I had never seriously considered marriage before. I called her up with the intent of proposing that night, of getting married as soon as possible. I asked her to have coffee with me, and she agreed. I imagined I would explain things to her over coffee, and she would understand and eagerly wed me. Then everything would be all right again.

I arrived early at the coffee shop because I couldn't stand to be anywhere other than in the bosom of salvation, which had not been Memphis, college, Old Gold cigarettes, literature, or a young woman from Spain, and therefore had to be matrimony with a somewhat plain girl I hardly knew. She was late, and while I was waiting for her a man sat down at the next table and struck up a conversation. He had a thin, harried face and wore a crisp denim shirt with pearl buttons on the pockets. His eyes were the same color blue as his shirt, and his eyelids seemed raw. He said he was thirty-five, worked in the television industry, and had just returned from L.A. All his friends were dying of AIDS. It was a terrible thing to watch someone dying of AIDS, he said. His boyfriend had just tried to run him over with his car. He thought he was losing his mind. He needed a shoulder to cry on.

My fiancée came in and rescued me. She was warm and pleasant and well rested. I got us coffee. I thought I'd start by asking if she liked living alone.

'You don't look very well,' she said.

'I haven't been sleeping.'

'I heard you quit school.'

'Yeah.'

'Why?'

I couldn't explain. The words *peanut-butter cup* came to mind.

'What are you going to do, go back to cruddy jobs?'

'Yeah, I guess so.'

'I don't understand.'

'I'll find my way.' I suddenly saw how ridiculous the idea of marrying her was. 'I'm leaving town,' I said.

'Where are you going?'

'I don't know.' I was convinced she would see that I was mentally disturbed, but she didn't seem to notice. We moved our mouths, talked aimlessly about writing, about likes and dislikes. I gave my speech about how college can teach only the consumptive side of literature. The gay man seemed to agree, but my ex-fiancée only regarded me with the familiar bland expression of the university dweller. I asked about her plans for the future. The gay man eavesdropped. We finished our coffee. I paid the check and walked her to her car through the crinkling, shimmering blue gloom.

When I'd said I was leaving town, I hadn't really thought about it. But my mind was so cluttered with thoughts of suicide I knew I had to leave. I have always believed that it is better to leave town than to take your life. Leaving town is a symbolic suicide, after which you get to make a new start, with the memory of all your previous lives. I borrowed a salt-devoured '64 Dodge Dart from a friend who seemed happy to be rid of it. He looked at me cheerfully and confidently, as if I knew what I was doing. I packed all my stuff and left behind the buckling walls and the fractured grocery store and the clock painted five minutes after three. I left at night, driving west, the direction of escape after disaster, the direction of decline and the setting sun.

All the time I drove I couldn't get suicide out of my mind. Self-destruction was the road behind, the road ahead, a black razor ribbon slicing out of the rearview mirror and straight through my scrambled brains. I felt nauseous, leprous, pickled, and raw. I felt as if I'd been wrapped in newspapers, lit on fire, and kicked all night by merry trick-or-treaters. I smoked the soothing ciggies, tapped the ashes out the window, watched the tumbling shower of sparks as I flicked the butts down onto the highway. I could feel my heart creaking and straining like the rotten mast of a mutinied ship on a stormy night. I stopped and peed behind some trees, looking up at the sky. My urine had a sharp smell, like musk ox and adrenalin. The sky was impersonally flat and godlessly bright.

In Lincoln, Nebraska, I stopped on an impulse to visit some friends, whom I hadn't seen in ten years. I stayed three days, and every evening we drank for auld lang syne, smooched and gargled and tackled each other around the neck with the crooks of our arms. A lonesome housewife from down the street showed up the second night. She had left her husband in Alaska for one feeble reason or another, and now she was a dental technician with a cheap apartment and two kids and sad blue eyes and a loneliness like a well in the ground with the splashing sound thirty seconds after you drop the rock. The third night, we ended up together, hopeless and drunk. It somehow seemed the best solution to our respective mires of failings, misdeeds, shortcomings, and itchy American insatiability. I hadn't been with a woman in a long time. I was mentally ill and drunk; she was desperate for kindness and attention. We each had a notion about getting something from the other: the love song learned about in childhood and believed in by the insane and the lonely, the chief cause of pain on earth.

Our little alcoholic tryst was a catastrophe. There was no love, only appendages and holes, and I could not function. My failure lowered the already dismal opinion I had of myself. I took my forty-foot hangover and my suitcase with the shirttail sticking out, kissed and shook hands all around, climbed back into my borrowed car, and limped away west.

I drove the length of Nebraska, stopping in little towns. At a grocery store in Hastings I bought apples and sardines. I went to look at the Little Blue River, then drove up to Willow Island to get a room for the night. The bedspread had pink pompoms, and there was a chrome Art Nouveau lamp on the nightstand. The whole room crackled in a bath of sterile white light. I switched off the lamp, got into bed, and stared up into the hissing, sleepless darkness. The blankets smelled like root beer and electricity and an old home permanent. I thought of suicide 1,287,000 times.

I left early the next morning. It began to snow around Lisco, along the Platte River; then the snow changed to rain. Somewhere, soon, I would have to make a stand. I tried to fight the feeling of futility, but it was as fixed and inevitable as the gray light of the sun through the clouds. I couldn't seem to put any distance between myself and failure. Wherever I went, it was always the same. There was no point in going on, no sense in prolonging the misery.

Scottsbluff is a cloudy, bleak town in the very western part of Nebraska. I got there around noon and found a motel for thirty-eight dollars a night. A red pickup truck and a blue Honda Civic were the only other cars in the lot. We were all in a row — Rooms 7, 8, and 9. My room was as bleak as the town. The windows were small, like jail windows, and filled with gray clouds. There was a strange little nook where the TV sat. I put my suitcase on the bed. The rain began to tick softly against the dusty windows.

I decided to wait until night. Night is the time to die.

The arms of the old killer are gentler then. I went out in the afternoon, bought a pack of Kools, and had my last meal at McDonald's: three cheeseburgers, small fries, small coffee, black. I felt sorry for myself, like a mother whose son is climbing the gallows stairs. I blubbered into my bandanna, mopped my eyes and face. The manager came over and asked if everything was all right. He was the first person to recognize that something was wrong—a perfect stranger. He asked if he could get me some more coffee. I said no and went back to the motel, where I sat in a chair and smoked the Kools one after the next.

When it was time to die, I took all the money out of my wallet and put it with a note on the corner of the dresser for the maid. Then I got down on my knees and prayed to God, asking him to forgive me for what I was about to do. The bed was high, and my elbows were way up there, as if I were once again eight years old and reciting the Twenty-second Psalm. Then I got up and fastened the plastic grocery bag from Hastings around my head, knotting it tightly like a bow tie at my throat. I stood in the middle of the room breathing in and out, the television on to cover any sounds of struggle. The plastic crackled and shrank and steamed up from the heat of my breathing. The blurry colors of the television flickered through the veil of the shrinking, then expanding, bag. Dying this way does not take long. The people who find you don't have to look at your face. I grew vaguely excited, euphoric. Then I yanked the bag off and threw it aside.

I left Scottsbluff the next day, skipping breakfast, and drove to Alliance, another bleak town, and then on toward Chadron, the next spot on the map. On the way to Chadron, just outside of Alliance, I stopped at a roadside attraction called Car Henge, a full-scale model of Stonehenge, except with old, silver-painted cars instead of stone monoliths sticking up out of the ground and stacked on top of each other. As a driver, I'd never stopped at a roadside attraction before. I was the only one there. It was cold and windy and gray. I got out and marveled at whatever Car Henge was: homage, science, art, burlesque. It was too cold to stand out there for long.

When I got back in the car, I was suddenly hungry. I had one apple and a can of sardines with chilies left. I peeled back the lid and poured the sardine oil into the very dry ground. A Winnebago rolled up next to me, and a bunch of kids tumbled out and dashed toward the ring of silver-painted automobiles. The sun came out for a moment and sparkled on the dust across my windshield. I sat with the car door open and the wind howling and ate the sardines. Somewhere long ago, in a place called Memphis, I had begun to lose my way. How had I come to value and believe in so many unimportant things, to fear and resist the life that was naturally mine? Down the road, in Chadron, a pretty little town of five thousand with snow still on the ground in May, a hotel cooking job and a shack for $150 a month awaited me. A few snowflakes started down. I ate the apple and watched the long, feathery slants come out of the sky.

La Calidad de la Vida

EVERY YEAR MY BACK GOES OUT. IT'S LIKE A SPECIAL anniversary, which I celebrate by groaning a lot and walking around like Groucho Marx with his tie caught in his zipper. This year it happens to me in Mexico, where I rent a large, brand-new, slightly leaky, four-bedroom house for sixty dollars a month in the medium-sized town of Jerez de García Salinas, about eight hundred miles due south of El Paso, Texas. The house, since I have only the upstairs, might better be classified as an apartment, but it is too big for me to call it that. The living room itself is larger than any apartment I have ever rented. The front patio is longer than the living room. My only furniture is an inflatable mattress, two plastic chairs with the Corona-beer logo on them, and a small plastic table. I have no TV, no radio, no telephone. I keep thinking I will furnish the place, but no money is coming in. I am living on money saved, and it is running out.

When my back goes out, there is little I can do about it. I have no diagnosis. I can't afford a doctor. It usually lasts three or four days. Sometimes I can barely walk; other times I can do a passable imitation of Charles Laughton in *The Hunchback of Notre Dame*. This time I can't even get out of bed. I have to use all of my imagination and many fabricated *tai chi* positions to find my way up after twenty minutes flopped out on my belly on the floor. An inflatable mattress might be a terrific swimming-pool accessory, but it is the last item on the list, just below 'tackle-football scrimmages,' for the maintenance of good back health. Gradually, with prayer and swearing and other types of secret guttural whimpering, I manage to make it to my knees. Then, with one bloodcurdling scream, I rise to my feet. Once standing, I can marionette myself about the room. A hot shower doesn't help (never does). It takes me another twenty minutes to put on my pants. I decide against shoes. After sitting in the chair for a while, I find I can't get back up, so I slide to the floor and crawl back into bed.

The next morning, it's raining. Between the middle of June and the middle of September comes the rainy season. The rest of the time it is bone dry and blue sky and enough dust from the unpaved roads to keep all the maids in Guadalajara busy for a lifetime. My back is no better. It takes me half an hour, grabbing window ledges and propping myself against walls and yelping like a little coyote pup, to stand. Fortunately, I am still wearing my pants. I look in the mirror; my left hip is kicked out like a freeze-frame photo of a hula dancer. I fry a quarter-pound of bacon and eat it with black beans and scrambled eggs, then go back to bed.

I dream and salivate and long like a love-struck teenager for blue, ten-milligram Valium tablets. From the time I was eighteen — when I first injured my back trying to lift eighty pounds of wienies off an electric cart and ended up in bed for four days — Valium has been the only agent, besides time, that can alleviate my condition.

To get Valium legally in the United States, you have to make an appointment with a physician, pay a minimum of sixty dollars for an office visit and prescription, resist the recommended battery of tests, and stare up into a face that doesn't trust you because you're probably a hypochondriac intending to file a malpractice suit; and by the time the appointment comes around, the problem has gone away by itself.

In Mexico, though you can supposedly buy anything you like over the counter, pharmacists are generally leery of a strange *gringo* asking for drugs often regarded as recreational, even if you stagger into the place in the shape of a pretzel. Besides, the *farmacía* is too far to walk while half paralyzed, and my Spanish is lousy. So I give up on the idea of Valium and decide to get drunk instead.

Putting on my shoes is no less formidable a task than placing both my legs behind my head. Laces flopping, I teeter about five hundred feet through the rain to my local *modelorama*, or liquor store. The signs in front of most Jerez liquor stores, including this one, say VINOS Y LICORES, even though ninety percent of these stores, including this one, do not sell *vino*. I have no explanation for this except that if you open a liquor store you must compete with all the other stores, which don't have wine either. I hobble into the small, open-fronted store and say hello to the girl who runs the place. She smiles and squints at me. Apparently, my Spanish sounds to her like a moronic Bavarian child in *lederhosen* talking after inhaling helium. The comedy is undoubtedly compounded by my crooked posture and untied shoes.

Whenever she gets the opportunity, the liquor-store girl nicks me for two or three pesos. She earns the minimum wage of thirty-five pesos a day (figure a peso to be roughly the equivalent of a dime), so, though it doesn't warm my heart to see her steal from me, I don't object. Lately, I have even begun tipping her, rewarding her for her dishonesty. This is a fainthearted and futile American strategy called 'reverse psychology.' To be honest, though, since I live on the rotund sum of ten dollars a day, I really don't mind supplementing her daily income of approximately $3.50. Today I buy a half-liter of *El Presidente* brandy (thirty-two pesos) and a pack of Benson and Hedges menthols (twelve pesos), tip her two pesos, say farewell in my baffling Spanish, and stumble back home with my goodies in the rain.

I drink the brandy slowly. I don't want to get drunk too fast, and especially don't want to throw up. (Kneeling at the toilet would be a hard position to maintain.) My power goes out three times, and after the third I just leave my digital clock blinking. The rain is leaking under the door, and a new water stain has appeared in the kitchen wall. I have already fixed one leak—crack in the skylight—with Elmer's glue. My brand-new house is also developing cracks along the walls and ceiling. The landlord has told me with no particular concern that the floor is weak. Few things in Mexico are built to last. Too many revolutions.

The brandy seems to help my back a little. It at least improves my mood—so much so that I begin to sing. My great, empty, cracked, leaky palace of a house has wonderful, haunting acoustics. I wish I knew some Gregorian chants. After I've sung all the songs I want to hear myself sing, I take a gulp of brandy and lie down flat on my back on the cold tile floor.

Late in the afternoon, my doorbell rings. My house is positioned like a fortress behind great, unscalable walls and two automatically locking black steel doors reminiscent of the entrance to a bank vault. This is typical for Mexico. Everything of value is shut up tight behind wrought-iron grating and roll-down metal gates and locked steel doors. There is little crime in this part of the world except for theft. Everyone in Mexico worries obsessively about being robbed. This is what happens when you've had your country stolen out from under you several times and you're still not sure if you're the fifty-first state of the Union, or a possession of Spain, or Chevrolet.

At the sound of the doorbell, I work my way deftly to my feet in about ninety seconds. I should be drunk; but it's amazing what agony and disfigurement will do for your faculties. The doorbell rings again. I flounder out the first metal door and crab my way down the stairs, certain that whoever rang will be gone by the time I make it down. I think my caller might be one of the three young local women who have begun to visit me in the evenings.

Mexicans are a very healthy people as a rule, but I sometimes wonder about the women's vision. Any American woman will tell you I am no catch — passive, poor, bland in appearance, and way too old (forty-three) to be on TV, except in a commercial for garden products or bran flakes. But these girls swoon and send me notes. They drop by in the evenings and ask me to translate things for them. Elva, who is eighteen, rings my doorbell in the daytime and dashes away. Seventeen-year-old Xenia, who adores John Lennon, arrives in a miniskirt with her guitar in hand to sing me Beatles songs. Margarita, twenty-one and stuck with a seven-month-old daughter, would like a husband who will not leave her. I have told them all that I have no money, but they still giggle and make eyes at me. They recognize that even as a cabdriver in America, my income would exceed the gross national product of Portugal. Most of the healthy, eligible Mexican men are working construction, factory, or restaurant jobs in L.A. or Chicago. Many of them will never return. The female-to-male ratio here is something like three to one, and any warmblooded, half-witted American bachelor between twenty and fifty arriving fresh from the States will feel like a sailor on the HMS *Bounty* landing on Tahiti.

When I open the door I find, not a pretty young Mexican girl standing patiently in the rain with a Backstreet Boys song for me to translate, but my friend Ismael. Ismael is sixty-nine and looks like Anthony Quinn. Though he was born thirty miles from here, he spent most of his life laboring in the U.S., and his English is excellent. As a U.S. citizen, he is entitled and desires to live in America, but like many others so entitled to and desiring, he doesn't have enough money. 'What's wrong with you?' Ismael says.

'My back is out.'

'Are you going to play poker?'

Though I decided earlier it would be impossible to play poker — not only because I can't sit for longer than ten minutes without becoming the Lincoln Memorial, but also because there is no one in the city of Jerez I know well enough to ask to tie my shoes for me — the brandy and the prospect of lying gnarled and fetus-like in an empty house staring at the spreading water stains on the walls have changed my mind. 'Just a sec,' I say, and I crawl back upstairs to grab my raincoat and bottle of brandy.

In my humpback state, I can't get into Ismael's old green Dodge pickup. My head won't clear the top of the door and the body won't bend without oaths issuing from the mouth. The rain keeps coming. Rainfall in the daylight hours, even during the rainy season, is unusual here. It almost always rains at night, to the delight of sleepers and corn farmers alike. I remain wedged in the truck's open doorway, my legs hanging out, getting wet. I need someone to come along and give me a good, swift kick. Finally, with a little howl, I manage to punch myself through. The girl in the *modelorama* watches me mildly, wearing her usual 'what is the *gringo* doing now?' look.

We drive through the sweet and peaceful little city, with its misty corn-tortilla and cooking-onion smells, past tiny corner grocery stores frozen in time and butcher shops with cow carcasses dangling in the windows and dozens of law offices with lawyers inside who have nothing to do. The police don't have much to do either (they need a few hundred thousand more laws to enforce, like their clever neighbors to the north), though every now and then they get to ride around in their patrol car with the siren on. A kid in a Mickey Mouse T-shirt strides toward us in the rain with a chicken under his arm. A dog with pointed, duct-taped ears barks at us from a rooftop. Ismael stops at a little store and buys two liters of orange pop.

We play poker at Les's house. Les was an international safety inspector and trouble-shooter before he retired to Mexico. He has many fascinating anecdotes about bulging railroad cars and exploding ammonia factories. A native of Oklahoma, he played football for the University of Alabama alongside Bart Starr, fabled quarterback for the Green Bay Packers. Les lives out on the edge of town on a dirt road with his little dog Lady in a house just slightly smaller than mine, for which he pays forty-five dollars a month rent.

Two more retirees, Joe and Tomás, are already seated at the table. Tomás, who is eighty, an ex-welder, ex-*pistolero*, and

San Francisco bar owner for thirty years, still remembers a sign in front of a Texas restaurant in 1943: NO DOGS OR MEXICANS ALLOWED. Though he pretends to be crusty, his pockets are always jammed with candy for the children. Joe, the quiet American from Boston, is threatening to move with his sister-in-law to Florida. We have been trying to talk him out of it, but he has been away from America too long and has forgotten about tollbooths, traffic jams, four-dollar cigarettes, school massacres, gangs, graffiti, and the 720 million NO PARKING signs.

I lean against the kitchen counter, take a slug of brandy, and watch Tomás unwrap a Bimbo *panqué*, or pound cake with nuts sprinkled on top. Bimbo is the name of a Mexican bakery whose products are similar to Hostess's. Joe is sipping a forty-cent Corona and smoking a Mexican cigarette called a *Boot*. Mexico might be the only place in the world where you can encounter two men at a table, one eating a Bimbo and the other smoking a Boot.

We draw cards to see who will deal. Ismael wins. I am equally in pain whether standing or sitting, so I sit. Whenever I stand up, I remain in the sitting position, barking at the table. This is amusing to my fellow poker players. Pain and grotesquerie are the two secret ingredients to good comedy. We play for five hours. It rains the whole time. The gods of luck smile down upon me. I can't reach the pots I have won. I struggle to deal the cards. Les gives me some kind of pill that I hope will prove synergistic with the brandy and knock me out cold, but it doesn't seem to help.

After the game Les, Ismael, and I go out to eat at a great restaurant with no name. The house specialty is *pozole*, a tomato-based soup with pork (usually from the head of the pig) and hominy, served with limes, chopped onions and lettuce, fresh oregano, and crisp corn tortillas, all for a dollar. The place is open only at night. The waitress is brusque and sweaty, just like an American waitress. A girl with Down's syndrome patrols the aisle all night, smiling and swinging her purse, just missing the heads of the customers.

I drape myself in the doorway and watch the rain come down. The streets are flooding. My sockless feet are soaked. Trini, the woman who makes the *pozole*, comes out from the back to say hello. She makes great *pozole* and is a sweetheart, but frowns constantly because she is puzzled by Americans who actually want to live in Jerez and come to eat at her restaurant twice a week. She says that she also had back trouble recently, and the doctor gave her a shot that fixed her right up. I ask Ismael if he knows a doctor. All I really want, I tell him, is some Valium. He says he knows a good doctor at a *farmacía* not far from my place and will take me there in the morning. Les orders a plate of *tacos de papas* — tacos filled with mashed potatoes. Ismael and I have the *pozole*. None of us gets hit in the head by a purse. Though I don't feel the slightest bit drunk, I tell the waitress I love her. The bill, including beer and cola and fifteen-percent tip, comes to less than five dollars.

The next morning I limp with Ismael over to the *farmacía*. He laughs at me and then apologizes, still grinning. He can't help it, he says. I tell him it's all right; maybe one day he will be in the hospital and I can come up to his room and laugh at him. The *pozole* is unquestionably a great hangover remedy. I feel as if I didn't drink a drop of brandy last night.

It's hot today, and I am sweating by the time we get to the *farmacía*, my left leg tingling and tired. The doctor is forty-five or so, a serious woman with gray streaks in her hair, who sits in the cool dimness behind her long glass counter. All around her are fascinating, nostalgic drugstore items — everything from notions and toys to little handmade dresses and cigarettes. My Spanish is not good enough to explain my problem, so Ismael fills her in. She nods, asking many questions, then comes out from the glass counter and lifts my shirt to poke around. She asks me if I have pain in my leg. I say I do. Then she goes into the back room and returns with an armful of drugs, including three syringes and six vials of something honey-colored. It looks for a moment as if I might have to take these needles home and stick myself with them. I explain that I can't give myself injections. This seems to amuse everyone. Then she takes me into the back room.

For all the drugs (no Valium, but a skeletal-muscle relaxant called Norflex Plus and some anti-inflammatory pills), the office visit, the three shots, and scheduled consultations over the next three days, the bill is twenty-five dollars. I may even have been given a diagnosis, but since my Latin is no better than my Spanish, I don't know what it is.

A few hours after the first shot, I am able to walk upright. By the second day, the knot of unruly back muscles has unsnagged, and most of the pain is gone. On the third day, I can do a one-and-a-half gainer with a twist off a thirty-meter springboard. I return to thank the doctor with an effusive gratitude she is probably accustomed to by now. Then I buy a pack of cigarettes, which she is happy to sell me. Where in America can you get your back fixed for twenty-five bucks and buy a pack of cigarettes from your doctor? This is what I love about Mexico: *la calidad de la vida.* The quality of life.

up, electronic gift cards, stamps and pierced earrings unless the item
faulty. This does not affect your legal rights.

Superdrug Stores plc
118 Beddington Lane, Croydon,
Surrey. CR0 4TB

Customer Relations
Freephone 0800 0961055

Superdrug ☆

REFUND EXCHANGES

We will happily give you an exchange or refund if you return the product in
its original, undamaged packaging in a saleable condition, with your
receipt within 28 days of purchase.
For the safety of all of our customers, we do not refund or exchange any
medicines, vitamins, baby food (inc milk), cosmetics, drinks, food, e top
up, electronic gift cards, stamps and pierced earrings unless the item is
faulty. This does not affect your legal rights.

Superdrug Stores plc
118 Beddington Lane, Croydon,
Surrey. CR0 4TB

Customer Relations
Freephone 0800 0961055

Superdrug ☆

REFUND EXCHANGES

We will happily give you an exchange or refund if you return the product in
its original, undamaged packaging in a saleable condition, with your
receipt within 28 days of purchase.
For the safety of all of our customers, we do not refund or exchange any
medicines, vitamins, baby food (inc milk), cosmetics, drinks, food, e top
up, electronic gift cards, stamps and pierced earrings unless the item is
faulty. This does not affect your legal rights.

Superdrug Stores plc
118 Beddington Lane, Croydon,
Surrey. CR0 4TB

Customer Relations
Freephone 0800 0961055

Superdrug ☆

REFUND EXCHANGES

We will happily give you an exchange or refund if you return the product in
its original, undamaged packaging in a saleable condition, with your
receipt within 28 days of purchase.
For the safety of all of our customers, we do not refund or exchange any
medicines, vitamins, baby food (inc milk), cosmetics, drinks, food, e top
up, electronic gift cards, stamps and pierced earrings unless the item is
faulty. This does not affect your legal rights.

Superdrug Stores plc
118 Beddington Lane, Croydon,

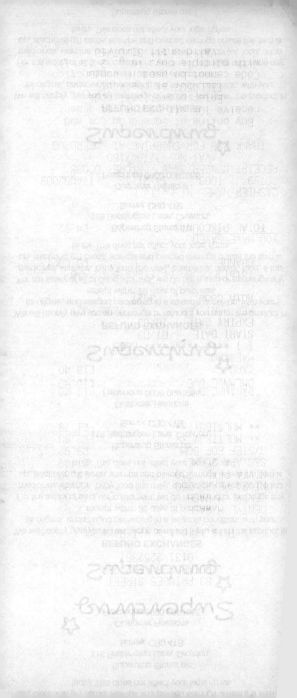

An Unfamiliar Form of Solitaire

WHEN I FIRST CAME TO THIS MOUNTAIN TOWN IN CENTRAL Mexico a year ago — bored and dissatisfied with myself and my American surroundings — I was eager to learn about a group of thirty or so *imigrantes*, American expatriates, who gathered daily in the lobby of the Hotel Jardin. I imagined these *imigrantes* to be desperadoes, dope dealers, derelicts, CIA operatives, war criminals, and colorful revolutionaries. I was somewhat disappointed to learn instead that every one of them was retired, a responsible pensioner, the very youngest fifteen years my senior. Nevertheless, *expatriate* being a polite term for *misfit*, I fit right in and made lasting friends all around.

On a Saturday morning in late February, my tenth month living in this town, I walked the mile from my house to the hotel in search of a poker game. Eight or nine *imigrantes*, armed with coffee cups, were assembled in the lobby.

I gestured to Esmerelda, our sweet-faced waitress, for coffee and took a seat next to Tomás, an eighty-one-year-old retired welder and bar owner from Arizona, who had just returned from three months in San Francisco, where it had rained the whole time and his daughter had kicked him out of the house.

'Thought there might be a poker game on,' I said.

Tomás turned toward Joe, who was sitting at a table against the wall with Jim, the retired archaeologist, and called out, 'Let's play tonight!'

Old Joe was a retired mapmaker, tall and rail-thin, with owl-like spectacles covering his frosty gray eyes. He shook his head. He did not like unscheduled events. An ex-Marine, he was almost ritualistic about his daily routine. His neighbors claimed they could set their watch by him.

'C'mon. I'll give you the money,' offered Tomás.

Joe lifted the *Reader's Digest* that he used as a lid to keep his coffee hot and took a sip. 'Monday,' he said.

I think Joe liked me, though you never knew for sure what he thought or felt, since he volunteered almost nothing about himself. He had a New England accent, but only by his license plates did I know he was from Vermont. He sat every morning at the hotel, gaunt and straight, hands on knees, offering little but the occasional dry joke. At noon, he went to lunch, then repaired to one of three bars, where he sat like a granite sculpture until dinner. He was not close to anyone. There had once been a woman who was going to join him in Mexico, but Joe had stopped talking about her two years ago.

Recently, Joe had surprised me by offering to get me some peyote. Ever since I'd read Carlos Castaneda's magic 'anthropology' books at age nineteen, I'd longed to try that granddaddy of psychedelics. I had sampled nearly every other drug of my generation, including forty types of LSD, 'green mescaline,' indolealkylamine-soaked table mushrooms (passed off as psilocybin), and methylene-dioxyamphetamine—all molecular imitations of mescaline, the active component in peyote—but the genuine article had always eluded me. Many people in the mountains of middle Mexico use peyote in solution to treat arthritis. It is also central in the religious life of the *Huicholes*, a local Indian tribe. I wondered if Joe had arthritis; he didn't seem the type to be experimenting with hallucinogens. He said the peyote would cost me five pesos, or about fifty-five cents. I imagined he had a *Huichol* source. I think he was going out of his way for me.

At a Super Bowl party a few weeks later, I saw Joe sitting at the kitchen table playing dominoes. He gestured me over and produced a plastic bag with what looked like a molded orange inside.

'Here's what you wanted,' he said.

'Thanks a lot,' I said, thinking it was a joke, somebody's lunch garbage. I wasn't thinking about the peyote. I gave the bag back.

About three weeks later, at a poker game, I mentioned the peyote to Joe again.

'I gave it to you already,' he said.

'What?'

'I gave it to you.'

'When?'

'At the Super Bowl party.'

'That was peyote?' I'd never seen peyote before, but I knew it came in 'buttons,' not big, moldy greenish balls.

'I told you it was what you wanted.'

'I didn't know it was peyote,' I said. 'Why didn't you say something?'

'What was I supposed to do?' he said. 'Advertise it to everyone?'

'Do you still have it?' I said.

'Sure. I'm using it for a doorstop,' he said.

On Monday Tomás and I drove over to Les's house at the edge of town for the poker game. Big Les was a retired safety inspector from Oklahoma who'd once been offered contracts by both the Canadian Football League and the Green Bay Packers. He was the last person you'd expect to see wearing a dress, but there he sat counting his pesos at the kitchen table with a slinky silk sarong wrapped around his waist. To the right of Les sat Ismael, a retired logger with dual U.S. and Mexican citizenship. He had recently totaled his truck on the way back from visiting his daughter in California, and now he had to wear a neck brace, though he could stand to have it on only about two hours a day. 'I hope you brought plenty of money with you,' he said.

'Deal the cards,' said Tomás.

For the first time in anyone's memory, Joe was late. The four of us kept turning our heads toward the door, listening for the squeak of the iron gate.

'Not like him,' said Ismael.

'Maybe we should go over and get him,' I said.

'No, he'll show,' said Les.

To the east, the sky grew dark and thunder rolled. Ismael drank two of my beers, so I walked to the store to buy more. The wind blew in stiff gusts that seemed to come from every direction at once. The air was heavy and damp. A flash of lightning split the clouds. Everyone in these mountains knows that when a storm appears to the east, it never rains. Also, rain in late February is rare in this part of the country. On the way back, I asked two men huddled along a cement wall if they thought it would rain. They said it would.

'I guess Joe is not going to show,' said Les when I returned.

'He probably forgot,' said Tomás.

'Too bad he doesn't have a phone,' said Ismael, peeling off his neck brace and setting it on the floor.

Raindrops began to tick against the dusty windows.

On Tuesday morning I went to the Hotel Jardin, and someone mentioned that there had been no sign of Joe since Saturday, three days ago. Concerned, Les and I drove over to Joe's apartment. Like many American expatriates, Joe lived alone. The windows were shut tight. His '89 Mercury Sable (with the Vermont vanity plates that read AMIGO) was parked out front, still splotched from the previous day's rainstorm. Les and I knocked on the door and tried to peer into the windows. We made more excuses for him. He's off on an excursion. He's met a little lady. He's on a drunk. He's at the cathouse...

'But what are the odds of any of these?' I said.

'Pretty slim,' Les admitted. 'Sometimes he goes to the border without telling anyone, but he would've taken his car...'

We talked to the woman who ran the little grocery store next door, where Joe went every day for cigarettes and beer. She, too, had not seen Joe for three days. She seemed worried. We knocked once more on Joe's door.

'Do you smell anything?' said Les.

'No, I don't think so.'

'I'll stop by later on tonight,' he said, 'and see if there's a light on.'

I said I would come by after school and check on him — I tutored local students in English at night.

'If he doesn't show up,' Les said, 'we'll come over in the morning and find the landlady.'

I walked away, my head filled with questions: What if he's inside and disabled? What if he's had a stroke, or slipped and broke his hip in the shower? How long would he last? What would he think of his friends laughing and sniffing indelicately outside the door? Why am I not doing something?

What if that was me in there? But then I thought: How many times have I let my imagination get the better of me? How many times have I thought the worst and been wrong?

It was a hot, sunny afternoon, February 29th, the odd day of the leap year. At my local grocery store I met a thirty-six-year-old man who was celebrating his ninth birthday. (He was technically younger than his seventeen-year-old son.) I drank two Victorias with him in honor of the Gregorian calendar reform. Then I bought a six-pack of Milky Way bars, a mango, a bag of limes, and three serrano peppers. It felt unusually good to be alive. On the way home I ran into Bob, a retired typewriter repairman and porno novelist, who was headed on his bicycle down to the town's only car lot. A road crew was just finishing up the four-laner out in front of my house, and a man roped horizontally to the tailgate of a slow-moving truck was using a spray gun to carefully lay a perfect coat of yellow paint over the new curbs. The air smelled dizzily of fresh airborne paint. Bob and I swapped a few toxic inhalant stories, marveled at the ingenuity of the road crew, and remarked that the city was beginning to look a little like Bakersfield.

'I heard Joe hasn't been to the hotel for three days,' Bob said.

'That's right,' I said.

'Not like him,' he said.

'Les and I went by his place today. Shut up tight. Car still out front.'

'Probably took off for Michoacán or something.'

'Probably did,' I said. 'Couldn't possibly be lying dead in there, listening to the rain…'

That night at school, I had a lull between two of my four scheduled students, so I went down to chat with Tomás, who sat in the plaza every evening and passed the time with Raymundo, the shoeshine man. When I told Tomás about Joe, he mentioned that Joe had a heart condition but refused to take his medication. A normal pulse rate is 60 to 80 beats per minute. Joe's was 110. He was also a heavy cigarette smoker. We both shook our heads. I lit a *Delicado*, a cheap but hearty Mexican unfiltered cigarette with sugar in the paper. Raymundo watched us intently, not understanding, but knowing something was wrong. I thought of the quote — I don't know who said it, maybe Santanaya: 'Americans do not solve their problems, they bid them amiably farewell.'

'He's probably dead,' said Tomás.

At eight o'clock, my last student canceled. On the way home, I stopped at Joe's apartment. The place was ominously dark, still shut tight, without the faintest sign of life. The car was still there. I knocked, waited, knocked again. I thought I smelled something now, though the neighborhood was always full of strong odors: the slaughterhouse was not far away; the 'river,' though dry, was essentially an open sewer; and the so-called Humane Society was constantly poisoning stray dogs, whose corpses were not always immediately recovered. I wondered if Les had been by yet. I knocked again and compiled another list of frail excuses.

I walked home distractedly, knowing that, whatever happened tonight, I would not sleep. My friend Ismael lived two blocks from me. I saw him sitting out front, visibly sore-necked and talking with his neighbors, Don Gavino and Don José. I went over and told them about Joe.

Don Gavino said, 'He lives alone?'

I nodded.

Ismael's neighbors began talking rapidly to each other about Americans who came to Mexico to live alone — something that was unthinkable to them, a disgrace reserved for *locos* and drunks. They talked as if living alone were a cause of death in itself. All the while, I was nagged by the thought of the possibility of Joe being alive, a dim spark in the darkness, a flutter of fingers, a moan.

'What are you going to do?' said Ismael.

I told him that Les and I were going over in the morning to find the landlady.

'Do you know who she is?'

'No. I think Les does.'

'I'll go over with you,' he said.

I stared at the ground for a minute. 'I think there's a chance that he might still be alive,' I said. 'If he's alive now, he probably won't be tomorrow.'

Ismael glanced at his watch. 'What do you want to do?'

'I think we should act.'

'It might be too late to find the landlady,' he said. 'We'll walk to the *Presidencia* and get permission to go inside.'

'Why don't you call the police?' suggested Don José.

A good idea, except I wasn't prepared to make it official, and besides, I didn't trust the police in Mexico. Any man who is paid the equivalent of two hundred dollars a month and is equipped with a gun in a country where graft is the rule and no one else is permitted to have firearms can only be expected to behave like a highwayman.

Nevertheless, we went into Ismael's house and called the police. The first three times, we got no answer. 'Of course. Who would ever need a policeman at 8:30 p.m.?' grumbled Ismael.

On the fourth try, we got through.

The police arrived in a brand-new white Ford F-250 pickup truck. I rode in the back, clutching the roll bar, the wind pressing back my hair. The cop in back with me asked, in Spanish, 'You live here?'

'I do.'

'Where are you from?'

'I was born in Denver.'

'Denver, California?'

'Denver, Colorado.'

'Oh.' He nodded with a kind of polite geographical indifference. 'Colorado.'

We were at Joe's two-bedroom apartment inside of two minutes. I hopped out and knocked on the green metal door again, certain that gaunt and imperturbable Joe would answer this time in his maroon terrycloth bathrobe and make a fool of me. The geographically indifferent cop grimaced and waved his hand in front of his face. 'The smell,' he said. I still thought the smell could be coming from elsewhere. The cops jabbered on their radios and interviewed the woman who ran the store next door. Neighbors appeared in doorways, arms folded over their chests. We crossed the street and rapped for ten minutes on the door of a neighbor who supposedly knew the whereabouts of the landlady. Roused at last, she gave us the address of the building's owners, who lived across town.

Two officers were dispatched to locate the owners and retrieve a duplicate key. I bought a package of *Delicados* at the store and stood with Ismael at the edge of the street. He was plainly distressed. Bad things happened to people who lived alone, and he lived alone too — one of several unfortunate habits he'd picked up during his thirty years in the States. 'I don't have the stomach for this,' he said, tugging down on the bill of his cap. I kept lighting up the *Delicados*. I was nervous because I knew that if Joe was dead, I would have to identify the body, and if he was dead, he had probably been dead for a long time.

A German shepherd patrolled the flat rooftop above Joe's apartment, barking at all the activity. (Barking rooftop dogs are a common presence in Mexico.) The crowd of spectators grew. A parade of police units passed by us, radios chattering. The geographically indifferent policeman explained to us that someone had been stabbed in a bar on the other side of town.

The building's owners were found, but no duplicate key. Ismael knew of a way into Joe's apartment from the rooftop, which was accessible through the store next door. Three policemen entered the store and appeared a few minutes later on the rooftop. I didn't believe they would get into Joe's apartment. Hours seemed to pass before one of the cops, a thickset man with a Stalinesque mustache, reappeared at the edge of the roof with a handkerchief over his mouth. He spit over the side. '*Esta muerto*,' he announced: he's dead. '*Esta in la cocina*': he's in the kitchen.

It should not have been a surprise. Where did I think Joe would be: sitting in a thatched bar in Mazatlán with a lovely divorcée from St. Bernard, Wisconsin? Another ten minutes passed before the lights went on in Joe's apartment. The front door burst open, and the three policemen exited, coughing and watery-eyed, as if they'd been gassed. They left the front door open. I felt lost.

The thickset policeman came over and described the scene to us: Joe had been sitting at the kitchen table doing his taxes—'Probably what killed him,' Ismael muttered—and had fallen somehow. There was quite a bit of blood on the floor. He had been dead for two or three days.

Now all the policemen drew notepads. They needed to know Joe's last name, age, marital status, occupation, nearest of kin, and so on. I was ashamed that I could answer none of their questions. I had talked to Joe on a hundred occasions, sat with him for hours at the hotel and at poker games and loner *gringo* picnics, and I'd never even learned his last name. I guessed that he was sixty-seven. I was fairly certain that he'd been born in Boston. I thought he'd flown a fighter plane in the Korean War.

Ismael didn't know the answers either, but he thought Les might. A policeman gave me a ride over to Les's house. Les lived alone too. His dog had recently been poisoned by the Humane Society, who distributed cyanide-laced meat to all dogs running loose on the street, sometimes even to particularly vocal rooftop dogs. Death by cyanide is violent but quick. To even the most discriminating dog, the cyanide smells sweet. Les didn't appear to be home. Probably dead, too, I thought. Then I saw the television glowing in the darkness. I knocked, and Les answered the door shirtless, buckling his pants over his big belly. 'What's going on?'

'Joe's dead,' I said.

'I knew it,' he said.

'I thought you might be able to tell the police who he is.'

The cop followed me inside. Les wrote Joe's last name on a napkin, then put on a shirt and went to get his shoes.

Les knew almost as little about Joe as Ismael and I did. The three of us stood in the middle of the street staring at the open door. By now there were a dozen cops, four or five emergency vehicles, and twenty or thirty bystanders gathered. A woman barely five feet tall appeared and began interviewing us. She had the collar of her jacket pulled up over her nose as if she were braving a Siberian snowstorm. At first, I thought she was a curious bystander, but she turned out to be the leader of the operation: the queen of the ghoul crew. She had an entourage of seven humorless plainclothes officers, one of whom had an automatic pistol stuck conspicuously down the front of his pants.

Hours passed. The air grew cold. The stars in the sky glittered like crushed blue ice. Countless cars, half of them with Texas or California plates, went by playing incongruent accordion-and-trumpet music. The door to Joe's apartment was still wide open. Most of the police officers assigned to the scene were sitting on the curb, smoking and talking among themselves. I gave up trying to understand what we were waiting for. Les and Ismael began telling jokes. Les rattled off several consecutive Martian jokes. I didn't laugh. 'What's the matter?' he said. 'Don't you like Martian jokes?'

'Our friend is lying in there dead on the floor,' I said. 'And you're telling jokes.'

'What else are you going to do?' he said.

A kid sailed by on a bicycle with a shining, metallic bag of chips in his teeth.

Ismael said that he thought Joe had a daughter.

'What if that daughter were here now?' I said. 'This is inhuman.'

'It's just Mexico,' said Les.

'I hope I die before my children do,' said Ismael.

The vehicle that was to take Joe to the morgue arrived around half past midnight. There was no indication that the investigating medical team would be any more expeditious than the droves of officials who'd preceded them. All of us, police, friends, and even the bystanders, were weary by now. We wanted to be done with it. Dust to dust. Call the daughter. Sign the death certificate. Hoist a farewell drink.

Sometimes I wonder if one of the functions of bureaucracy in such cases is to numb the bereaved.

Joe was in ghastly shape. He lay on his side under the empty bird-cage of Sonny, his songbird, who had died two months before. I had seen corpses before, but never one ripened three days in a warm, shut-up room. The smell was overpowering. Photographs were snapped, examinations made, and more reports filled out. Les battled for Joe's wallet — he knew it was unlikely that the money would be returned — but the queen of the ghoul crew insisted the police retain it. It would be returned, she assured us. (And it was, *sans* sixty-five dollars.) While the medical team worked on Joe's bloated body, we sorted through his belongings looking for letters, address books — anything on which a relative's name might be found.

Finally, the body was loaded into the wagon for transportation to Zacatecas, the state capital, where an autopsy would be performed and the body stored in a freezer until we could notify the next of kin. Since Ismael was a native, he took legal responsibility for settling Joe's affairs in Mexico. We decided to call the relatives in the morning. It was almost 2 a.m. Joe had been dead for three days. Another day wouldn't matter.

On Wednesday morning, we notified Joe's girlfriend, the closest person to a relative listed in his nearly empty address book. This was the woman who had promised to come live with him in Mexico. She didn't seem surprised at the news. Then came the warm gleam of sadness in her voice. She said Joe had a surviving brother and sister, neither of whom he'd been close to. He had also once been married, but that was long ago and there was no sign of an ex-wife. The girlfriend said she would notify everyone concerned and get back to us about the arrangements. She had never even come to visit him, though they had lived together in Vermont for seventeen years.

When we went to the hotel that morning, almost everyone had already heard the news, but the story was oddly altered. Leti, the hairdresser, who lived across the street from Joe, had called her American client, Iris, and the brushfire of thrilled and inaccurate information had spread from there: Joe had bled to death. I was the one who had climbed down through the rooftop and discovered the body. A passerby had recognized me among the throng of police and reported that I had been arrested. I would not have been surprised to hear that I was the prime suspect in the case.

For those who hadn't heard the news, the first question was: how did he die? We said we didn't know—we were waiting for autopsy results—but we were fairly certain it was a heart attack or a stroke. He had probably died instantly. We attempted to minimize the amount of blood, any suggestion of struggle, and the state of decomposition. It's all right to lie when painting the last scene for friends.

The mood was somber at first, a kind of pallid, labored clapping of the eyelids. You could almost see the inward mortal thoughts of Joe's fellow *gringos*, all of them retired, all far from home, many living alone: should I move back in with my children in Austin? Should I swallow my pride and marry that old girl in Los Alamos? If I died or fell in my kitchen, how long would it take for someone to find me?

But, gradually and steadily, the mood improved. News of the death of someone well known but not terribly close is often vitalizing: Old Joe is gone, but I live on. Gary, a retired newspaper editor who had recently decided to return to the U.S. for surgery on a cyst that he was certain was cancerous, began to laugh. His big teeth glittered. His eyes danced with light. Gary laughed because he had thought it was his turn. Joe had died in his stead. Joe had died for us all. There was much levity all around, the energy of the blood sacrifice.

The girlfriend called back that afternoon and said she would be flying down. Les described the three options for disposition of the body: shipment in coffin to the States, which might cost as much as ten thousand dollars and take as long as six months; local burial, the conventional choice; or cremation, which was almost unheard-of in Mexico. We needed to move soon, he said, before the state took Joe's body. A state burial, he explained, was not desirable.

For the rest of the day Les, Ismael, and I lingered behind the tall gates of bureaucracy in various unlabeled rooms where teams of typists hammered away under high white ceilings, taking down the same information the cops had gleaned from us over and over in triplicate the night before. It was almost dark by the time the carbon was pulled from the last typewriter, but we had hardly begun. We had no death certificate, no medical report, no documentation of authority for the disposition of body or belongings—nothing really but a *Delicado* headache and a firm distaste for ever dying. The three of us drove to a good restaurant with fifty unoccupied tables. Ismael said the dinner was on him. My friends' faces were radiant, like those of lost boys gathered round a campfire in a dark forest. I could not help but admire the man in his immaculate cook whites working busily among the shining pans, so happy that we had come to eat in his empty restaurant. Les told a joke about a disgusting baker. The punchline was: 'You think that's bad, you should see him make doughnuts.'

'Why do the Americans always live alone?' said Ismael.

'Because relationships in America are impossible,' I said.

'They're not impossible,' Les said. 'I've been married three times.'

The next morning we went over to clean up Joe's apartment in anticipation of the girlfriend's arrival. The kitchen smelled like a butcher shop. The blood, about a pint's worth, had hardened in a brick-colored puddle on the tile floor. Les reached down, plucked Joe's red-dipped spectacles out of the dried pool, and set them on the microwave. Except for the spilled blood, the place was very neat. There was a solitaire game, of a form unfamiliar to me, in progress on the glass-topped kitchen table. The face-up cards were all clubs and spades.

We emptied the refrigerator: a jar of strawberry *mermelada*, a quart of milk, sliced hard salami, *Fud* (pronounced 'food') brand hot dogs and bacon, smoked *chuletas* (pork chops), about two pounds of good ground Veracruz coffee, a package of individually wrapped American cheese slices, some curling-from-age corn tortillas, a moldy piece of cheese, two withered red apples, a small plastic bottle of Thousand Island dressing, a packet of Blue Ice. No peyote.

I filled a bucket of water, poured in half a cup of Clorox, and began to mop at the blood, which behaved as if it were dried red paint. Les and Ismael returned to municipal headquarters to joust with the civil servants. Tomás showed up and rummaged disinterestedly through Joe's belongings. Tomás's two best friends had died recently, six days apart, one in similar circumstances to Joe (it had been five days between death and discovery), and he seemed only weary of death. I poured one bloody bucketful of bleach water after another down the kitchen sink, managing to spill some on my shorts. After the mess was cleaned up, I began to look idly about for the peyote, not stating my intentions to Tomás; I didn't want to look like a scavenger. I surreptitiously peeked in hats and boots and plastic containers. I sifted through drawers. No luck.

A few vultures flapped around the open front door. 'Any items for sale?' they inquired.

I set the box of groceries outside.

Later that day we learned that the girlfriend was not coming after all. Ismael was given power of attorney, by fax from the brother, to dispose of Joe's worldly possessions, which were: a stove, a small refrigerator, a microwave, a small television set, a bed, an outboard motor, an '89 Mercury

Sable, a glass-topped kitchen table and chairs, and miscellaneous tools, books, clothes, and household goods. Ismael assured the brother that the sale price of the car would cover the cost of the funeral. More power of attorney contracts were faxed. A will was discovered: Joe had requested that his ashes be scattered over a lake in Middleton, Vermont.

On Friday morning the medical report finally appeared. Cause of death was listed as myocardial infarction (heart attack) compounded by atherosclerosis (Marlboro Lights and *Fud* hot dogs).

Shortly after noon we drove to the capital city of Zacatecas, about forty-five minutes away. It was a crisp, bright blue day. Zacatecas, half again as high in altitude as Denver, Colorado, is reminiscent of San Francisco, with its steep, winding, narrow streets. The crematorium was a sprawling new facility, as empty as a funeral parlor on the moon. The proprietor gave us a short tour, informing us that the ovens alone had cost one hundred ninety-three thousand to build. (I wondered if he meant pesos or dollars.) He said there had been only a hundred cremations in the last two years, about one a week. Despite the Pope's reluctant stamp of approval, Mexicans were still pretty cool toward cremation, the proprietor said, but Catholic sentiment and Mexican tradition would probably change. Especially, I thought, since it's only three hundred bucks, total package.

We followed the hearse through the hilly, crowded streets to the morgue, which was heavily guarded by smirking plain-clothes officers who seemed to enjoy telling us we could not enter. 'All we want is a dead body,' we said. They told us to park up the hill while they let the hearse through. Joe, who had supposedly been stored in refrigeration (I'd pictured a nice, clean drawer, tag on left toe), had been dropped on the tile floor like an old bowling trophy, seemingly unmoved since the day they'd transported him. Badly distended, he was balloon bellied and toad black. His nearly severed tongue lolled out the side of his mouth, probably the origin of all the blood. His bulging, frosty eyes were almost colorless. None of the policemen was interested in helping us load him into the hearse. There is nothing on earth to match the smell of a decomposing human going on the seventh day.

The proprietor of the crematorium told us it would take four and a half hours to incinerate the body. Les asked if it would be possible to retrieve Joe's Marine Corps ring. As a piece of jewelry, it was virtually worthless, but Les thought it might be important as a memento. The proprietor explained that the ring could not be removed because of the advanced state of rigor mortis. Les suggested that the finger be cut off. The proprietor said he was not in the habit of mutilating corpses.

'You're going to turn him into a pile of ashes anyway,' Les said.

The proprietor shrugged.

Whatever is left of that ring probably lies in brass beads at the bottom of a lake in Middleton, Vermont.

Late Saturday morning we returned for Joe's ashes. They were in a square, brown, wood-grain polystyrene box, like something from Radio Shack. Joe weighed about eight or nine pounds, all told. I considered all the cremation scams that had been uncovered lately by war-starved investigative journalists. Whose ashes were these really? But then again, what difference did it make? Ashes are ashes. The real Joe, the quiet, dry-witted retired mapmaker and ex-Marine from Vermont, was already long gone.

On the ride back, I thought about how little Joe and I had in common. Our age, tastes, geography, and background were all different. But one day someone would probably find me sprawled over a table in a motel in North Dakota, or swollen like a blackberry on the floor of a hut in Thailand, one more cold, dead American, alone and far away from home.

On Sunday we sorted and divided Joe's belongings. The apartment now smelled only cheesy. As legal executor, Ismael took Joe's car, microwave, refrigerator, camera, and tools. Les grabbed the stove, color TV, outboard motor, and two harmonicas with instruction books (*How to Play the Harmonica in One Hour with Your Eyes Closed*, or whatever). Mel, retired electrical engineer, showed up with a truck and some helpers and got his furniture back and also took the glass table and chairs.

I, the superstitious, took nothing. The idea of deriving benefit from someone's death seemed distasteful. I wanted only the peyote, which was technically mine, anyway. I intended to write an account of Joe's passing entitled: 'Essay Written on a Dead Man's Peyote,' a magical *memento mori* that, even if it wasn't any good, might succeed by virtue of its title alone. I was still convinced the peyote was somewhere in these rooms, carefully hidden, a little ready-made packet of unrevealed truth.

'Seems a shame to leave all this stuff to the buzzards,' Les said to me. 'At least you knew him. Don't you need anything...?'

I did need razor blades, which were expensive in Mexico. And I took the razor, because mine was shot. After that, it got pretty easy: a radio/cassette player, a stack of towels, a twelve-pack of toilet paper. I also grabbed a five-gallon water bottle and Joe's beautiful Indian-blue fleece pullover (made in Taiwan, washing instructions in Spanish), which I thought I would give to my father. Most of Joe's books were westerns or adventure novels, but there were a few exceptions: an anthology of Latin American short stories; *Death Ship*, by B. Traven (who wrote *Treasure of the Sierra Madre*); and *The Old Gringo*, by Carlos Fuentes, a novel prophetically punctuated by the line: 'The Old Gringo came to Mexico to die.' I put all this but the water bottle in two American Tourister suitcases, which I imagined would come in handy when I moved, as usual, in a few weeks.

After that I went home and sat alone in my rooms among the inventory of a dead man's belongings. 'Any man's death diminishes me,' John Donne wrote. Especially after you make a cheap run on his personal effects, I thought. I was unimpressed with myself, as usual, and after a while I went to bed, which is what people who live alone often do in the middle of the day. I was tired and fell asleep easily. I had a dream that I found the peyote in one of the suitcases. The 'button' was chocolate covered and packed with useful fortune-cookie phrases, none of which I can remember. Then Old Joe came to me out of a river of fog. He was spectrally thin and dressed like a parson, and he had a stack of maps under his arm. He was 'in a hurry to get to work,' he said, but he wanted to let me know that everything was all right. 'How are they treating you?' I asked, but he just nodded, already fading. I managed to scribble down some of what was written on the maps under his arm: secrets of the realm beyond. I put the scrap in my left pocket. When I woke up, all the windows in my house were dark.

Things I Like About America

WHEN I GOT BORED WITH MYSELF IN KANSAS, I DECIDED I WOULD move to a place that ended in the letter O. After ruling out Idaho, Puerto Rico, Morocco, and Trinidad and Tobago, I finally narrowed the list down to Ohio and Mexico. Then I asked all my friends — and even some people I didn't know — whether I should go to Mexico or Ohio. They all agreed it should be Ohio. In Mexico, they assured me, I would get thrown into a stone prison, acquire an incurable stomach virus, and get caught in the middle of a revolution. *Cholo* racists would drown me in a sewer. The police would confiscate everything I owned. Everyone had a Mexican horror story.

Mexico was wonderful, by the way. I stayed in the mountains of Zacatecas for a year and fell in love with the people. The only problem was, I ran out of money. So, like almost everyone else in Mexico, I had to go to the U.S. to find a job.

Ohio still seemed like a good choice. I picked Zanesville off the map. It was the right size — big enough for jobs to be plentiful, small enough to negotiate by foot — and not too close to the wino- and pigeon-cluttered shores of the Great Lakes. Quirky and peaceful West Virginia, which even John Denver couldn't make popular, was only a stone's throw away. Zanesville had a kind of crazy sound to it. 'Where is Poe anyway?' 'He is in *Zanes*ville, man.'

My good friend and *compatriota*, Les, a big man with a white mustache and a great affection for crunchy Mexican Cheetos, offered me a ride to Wichita, where he was going to visit his mother, who no longer recognized him.

It took a day to make the border. We dropped down out of the mauve-and-violet-stained Sierra Madres Occidental. It was early April, the best time of year to travel. The roads were virtually empty. The air was clear and cool. Many glass trucks had toppled on the tight turns, leaving island strands of hazy green rhinestones across the sand, and I saw a bird fly out of the side of an entirely hollow cow lying on the edge of the road. Somewhere in San Luis Potosi we ran over six nuns, one of them alligator-faced, another carrying a brass walking stick. They flew up over the hood like magic crows. A few miles later we had to stop for a towering shadowed monk. That part might have been a dream. I had taken a raspberry-flavored travel sickness pill that made me drowsy. But Mexico is rife with spirits. This is because people believe in them. In the middle of the desert we stopped for *huevos rancheros* and cold instant coffee at a truck-stop restaurant filled to every window with the living branches of a single giant tropical tree.

We crossed the border at Nuevo Laredo. One of the first things that struck me, after being out of the U.S.A. for a year, was how many people were dressed up like bikers, potbellied in chin beards and earrings and ponytails, death-theme tattoos on their arms, and Harley Davidson T-shirts, even some of the men. This must be the urban tribalism counterculture anthropologists predicted, a nation organized against itself, a society almost entirely composed of pretend rebels and outsiders whose plaintive cry is 'I don't belong!'

In Cotulla, Texas, Les and I spent the night in an 'executive' motel: hair dryer, large-screen TV, ironing board, coffeemaker, and basketful of exotic toiletries. This is the new face of upscale franchise America. Poor people need not apply.

I started a list of things I like about America. It went:

1. *Toilet paper in the public restrooms.*

2. *Roads without holes your car can fall into.*

3. *Decent wages.*

I couldn't think of any more.

'Readable street signs,' offered Les.

'Right.'

'And water you can drink out of the taps without getting cholera.'

'And they don't charge you to pee in the restrooms,' I added with sudden patriotic inspiration.

'In America,' he agreed, 'you can pee for free.'

The next day we drove through Pecan Bayou, which was not a bayou but more of a creek with maybe a few pecan trees somewhere. All along the highway, the bluebonnets were in bloom like fine sprays of xylophone music for the eyes. Add bluebonnets to the list of things I like about America.

For two nights we stayed in the more practical Holiday Motel (not too far from the windmill museum) in Les's hometown of Shattuck, Oklahoma, which like many small towns in the South and Midwest is dying. Les needed to pick up prescriptions and I wanted to try some of the canned beer there. Les drove me around a wheat farm looking for mastodon bones he had discovered years before, but the bones were gone, plowed back under by the farmer. Every morning we went for breakfast at Ed's, which had recently become Conita's, though Conita's husband had taken up with a seventeen-year-old girl and made her head cook, so Conita had gone to Woodward thirty miles away, which was why everyone still called the place Ed's. One of Les's childhood buddies thought he could get me a job for eight dollars an hour chroming fixtures for oil-rig machinery. I considered staying, but this was Les's town, not mine.

IN SUNNY, COOL WICHITA I SAID GOODBYE TO LES AND BOUGHT a ticket for Zanesville, my voice booming as if I'd grown up there and was returning home after twenty years in the army with a purple heart to run my father's grocery store.

What kind of trip will this be? I thought as I boarded the bus. As soon as I took my seat, the guy behind me answered my question by dropping his suitcase out of the overhead rack onto my head. The bones in my neck made a sound like a handful of celery being snapped in half. His girlfriend laughed.

'Jesus, I'm sorry,' he said. 'Are you all right?'

'No,' I said, swimming in and out of consciousness, a ring of shattered blue and green stars orbiting my head.

His girlfriend continued to snicker.

'I am really, really sorry, man.'

'That's all right,' I said, wondering if I had the balance to stand up and punch his girlfriend in the nose. 'Just be glad it didn't hit me somewhere vital.'

Then, just before St. Louis, it began to rain. I was watching the goldfish in the window and humming that B.J. Thomas classic 'Suitcases Keep Falling on My Head' when Robert Duvall appeared without warning to my left. It wasn't Robert Duvall but it looked a lot like him. He was chalky and bald with crooked teeth and wounded dark blue eyes, and he was metabolizing alcohol in great sour gusts. I had met him in the Kansas City depot where we had one of those intellectual exchanges that are only possible standing in line waiting for a bus to St. Louis. Duvall was a bona fide alcoholic drifter who stayed in cities only weeks. He'd just been to Sacramento for 'a hundred days,' and was headed to New England, he said, 'to see if the people were different.' He was forty-six years old and claimed to have read thirty-five thousand books. He was a Freudian, a Darwinist, a logical positivist, a neo-Luddite, and a follower of the French utopian socialist reformer Charles Fourier. No wonder he drank.

He plopped right down on my glasses, which I had set aside so I could sleep.

'Hello there,' he said, wilting me with a blast of toxic liver fumes. 'I hope you don't mind. I was interested in what you were saying before about the external directive force that we may mistakenly describe as space.'

'You sat on my glasses,' I said.

'What?'

'Stand up. You're sitting on my glasses.'

He stood up and looked back between his shaky knees like a shortstop that had just let an easy one get through. There were no glasses.

'Where are my glasses?'

'I don't know,' he said.

I had no spare glasses. My neck was broken and now I was blind. Everything looked like a runny Manet in the rain. This is how people become homeless, I thought, a can full of nickels between their legs.

'Here they are,' piped the woman behind me, handing them over, slightly mangled.

I set them on my nose, where they hung like a surrealist painting.

The rain streaked down, solid, ceaseless, and gray: Missouri, Illinois, Indiana. The sappily phrased Terry Jacks song 'Seasons in the Sun' ran round and round in rusty carousel through my baggage-addled brain, while Duvall expounded on celestial mechanics, the neurochemistry of love among the *Homo sapiens*, and a particular Kansas City bar, which he'd found in walking distance from the depot and where he'd tried to become part of everyone's life by demonstrating his intellectual superiority. He couldn't understand why the *Homo sapiens* had jeered him ('Why, if I met someone who'd read thirty-five thousand books,' he said, boring into me with his wounded, dark-blue eyes, 'I would be in awe of them').

Duvall finally left me in Indianapolis. I think he needed alcohol. He had begun talking about suicide. The woman behind me leaned forward as he was walking away and said, 'I sure feel sorry for him. He seems so bright...'

It was still raining when the bus pulled into Zanesville at seven o'clock that night. I got a little sick dip of dread in my stomach when I saw the sign out on the freeway: *Zanesville*: *Next Four Exits*. Which meant that the city was the only thing it couldn't be: TOO BIG. But I conned myself into thinking it would work. I looked for a motel on the way in and saw none.

I was the only passenger to get off in Zanesville. The depot was not downtown but on the edge of the suburbs, at the terminus of the city transit system. The ticket window was closed. I strolled aimlessly about the unoccupied depot, my neck making splintery broken-glass noises as I swiveled my head. A man in a bus driver's outfit stepped from a doorway.

'Excuse me,' I said. 'Is there a motel nearby?'

He squinted at me. 'What kind of motel you looking for?'

'Cheap motel.'

'Aren't any of those left,' he said, puffing up indignantly. 'They bulldozed 'em all down.'

'Well, what do they have left?'

'They're all out by the interstate. Got a Ramada.'

'That's seventy bucks a night.'

'Well,' he said. 'There's a Travel Lodge not far from here. That's probably the cheapest one we got.'

'That sounds good. Where is it?'

'About three miles from here. Hold on a second. I'll give you a ride.'

He drove me through the rain in his empty bus, chatting affably about the city, which was discouragingly big, approximately the size of Iraq. And I was not sure if I wanted to stay here and try to find a job, but I needed a shower, a large beer, a chance to sleep horizontally, and a few moments with the Weather Channel just to see out of curiosity if there was somewhere in the world where it was not raining.

The cheapest motel in town was forty-five a night, blow dryer, ironing board, coffeemaker, twenty-four-inch cable TV, basketful of exotic toiletries. You get the little magnetic card now instead of a metal key, and the cost of the towels stolen from your room the night before is also figured into your bill. My cervical vertebrae felt cracked like fine brandy snifters and I was still seeing stars. There was an ache in my left arm that only went away when I dropped my chin to my chest. Some kind of paralysis was setting in, irreversible nerve damage. I took a hot shower and changed my clothes, and went out to explore the city streets before it got dark.

Zanesville was not right at all. The downtown area was gutted, a ghost town in the rain. Turning back toward the freeway, I stumbled onto a Wendy's and a gas station, where I picked up a local newspaper. They also had big cans of cold beer, which you can add to the list of things I like about America. I ate a couple of fish-fillet sandwiches and managed to ruin my sweatshirt with a blob of tartar sauce. When I opened the paper to the classifieds, I saw that the rent was too high. There were also no residential motels or furnished rooms—nothing but unfurnished apartments: first and last months' rent and security deposit in advance. I'd have to work two months full time just to get into an apartment with no furniture and the neighbors upstairs practicing the Texas two-step all night.

As I watched the Weather Channel in my motel room that night (what is it costing me to stay here, about six dollars an hour?), I tried to think of a place to go next. It was snowing like the last day in hell in Michigan and Wisconsin, both of which I'd vaguely considered as alternatives. Then I began to ponder Fond du Lac, the idyllic small-town setting of a Delano-Roosevelt young adult romance called *Seventeenth Summer*, which my friend Sara reads faithfully every year. The choice seemed preposterous enough. Logic certainly hadn't gotten me anywhere. And what better place for a middle-aged man who refuses to grow up than the setting of a young adult romance? I snapped off the TV, finished my beer, and turned out the lights.

The next morning it was snowing in Ohio. I carried my bags the three miles back to the depot, over a rusting bridge across the swollen, racing, tea-and-cream-colored Muskingum River.

The Greyhound office was open. A young woman, who was also the dispatcher for the city transit system, stared at me. 'Can I help you?'

'I'm not exactly sure where I'm going yet,' I said. 'But I need a bus ticket.'

She nodded, eyes flicking off to the sides, wondering what number to call.

'Do you go to Fond du Lac, Michigan?' I said.

'Let me check,' she said, entering the name into her computer. 'No,' she said. Then she thought for a moment, stooped to pick up a book, leafed through it, and set it back down. 'Do you mean Fond du Lac, WISCONSIN?'

'Yes, that's the one.'

'Do you want a ticket?'

'Yeah, why not? One way. Do you know anything about it?'

She shook her head.

'I've never been there before,' I said.

'Are you sure you want to do this?'

'I think it's snowing up there,' I said.

'I've never had anyone do this before,' she said.

'You never had anyone buy a ticket to Fond du Lac?'

'No, I never had anyone come in here who didn't know where they were going.'

TWO DAYS LATER, THE BUS DROPPED ME OFF AT THE HARDEE'S in Fond du Lac, which didn't look much like the idyllic setting of a young adult romance, but at least it had stopped snowing. I cupped a flame and lit a smoke. The sign out on the highway had said: *Fond du Lac: Next Four Exits*, so I was still a little nauseated. But, coming in, I'd also noticed an old motel called the Fondy — probably twenty-five a night. A small sign of life. A little glimmer of hope.

I dragged my bags into the Hardee's, piled them against the wall, and ordered a couple of breakfast croissants. The teenage girl who waited on me was enormous (largely German, I expect) but very friendly. I asked her a few questions about the town, how big it was and that sort of thing. She shouted to one of her coworkers to come over and they stood before me and performed a complicated shrugging ritual. *I don't know*, they took turns saying. They were both baffled by every physical aspect of their hometown, except to agree that it was dull and that I should get out, maybe go to Eden, a small town to the south.

'Can't go back to Eden,' I said.

They tipped their heads at me.

'Can I get a job in Eden?' I asked them. 'Do they have jobs in Eden?'

'Oh, no. Of course not.'

'Well, I need a job.'

'Well, you should stay here then.'

I bought a paper and read it while I ate my croissants. Many jobs. Rent a little high. Rooms for rent. But Fond du Lac was a huge town, even bigger than Zanesville. I was picking cities that sounded like planets and being rewarded with planet-sized cities. Everything would be two miles away every time I walked out the door. By the restroom was a map of Wisconsin, which I studied for a minute. I had enough money to make a small jump, maybe Appleton, the birthplace of both Houdini and the John Birch Society (that's an energetic combination), but I was beginning to get this feeling that Appleton wouldn't be much different from Fond du Lac: *Appleton: Next Four Exits*. And pretty soon, very soon—maybe like now—it would be time to stop throwing away my money.

So I wandered on down to the Fondy Motel, only a couple of blocks from the Hardee's. It looked perfect: quiet and neat, circa 1951, a weekly rental, with tree shade and thick plaid blankets on the beds and knotty wainscoting and the smell of upside-down pineapple cake. I'd buy a week or two here, sleep for a day, then get serious about finding work. But a handwritten sign in the office window said: *No one in office, no vacancy*, even if there were only two cars in the lot.

And from what I could gather, the rest of the motels were crammed against the highway, along with the chain restaurants and the strip mall, four or five miles away. And I was not about to walk four or five miles with these suitcases to stay in a Ramada Inn for seventy dollars a night.

So I opened the paper to the rooms for rent. There were two that looked about right: one for $190 a month, and another for $260 a month—too high, but still cheaper than a weekly motel.

A convict was using the pay phone. The wind was blowing hard and cold. I imagined it was like this most of the time along Lake Winnebago, the wind blowing hard and a convict on the telephone. The convict had a mouth like a boot-camp latrine. He seemed to be proud of the fact that he had just gotten out of jail. His car was a wreck. I stood there in the cold wind waiting for the phone, newspaper flapping all around me. I waited about five minutes. He was scrunched down against the wind, croaking invectives into the mouthpiece. Finally he saw me and scowled.

'You waiting for the phone?'

'Take your time,' I said.

'How long you been waiting?'

'Not long.'

'Why didn't you say something?' he said, immediately hanging up.

'Finish your call,' I said.

'Ahhh,' he growled, swatting the air. Then he saw my bags piled up on the lawn. 'What are you doing?' he said.

'Trying to get a room.'

'You want a ride?'

'If I knew where I was going, I would.'

'Where's the room at?'

I showed him the ads.

He nodded, scratching into his spiky blond beard. 'OK,' he said. 'I'll give you a ride if you're still here in half an hour.'

He jumped into his ramshackle car, nodded at me, and clattered away.

The room for $190 was taken, so I called the only one left. A woman answered. It was still available.

'I'm just in town,' I said. 'Can you give me directions?'

'Where are you?'

'The Hardee's on Main.'

'OK, well, you go north on Main. It's just past First, about twenty blocks.'

I scribbled down the address.

'Be sure to come around the side,' she said. 'Not the front.'

FOND DU LAC IS ESSENTIALLY ANYWHERE, U.S.A., AN automobile town, spread out as far as possible, littered with broken beer bottles and fast-food trash, and populated with obese and unhappy people dressed up like bikers and pirates. The ethnic composition is about eighty-percent German, I am told. A few Irish slipped in. The local Indian populations were all rounded up, disenfranchised, and forced into gambling casinos. The French trapped some beaver, as they are wont to do, left their recipe for fries, and moved on.

As I carried my bags up Main Street, people yelled at me from their cars: 'Get a job!' 'FUUUUUCK!' 'Your mother is a rottweiler!' This yelling is an odd custom I have encountered all across the U.S. These are the voices of an angry and frightened society, the 'No Fear' society, a jaded and profane society. The seagulls swarmed overhead on the sharp lookout for abandoned bacon cheeseburgers. I passed three cheese-pale youths dressed for a funeral, who had so much jewelry punched into their faces I feared they were in danger of being carried off by birds.

The rooming house was something out of a Shirley Jackson novel—a great brown Victorian funhouse, circa William Howard Taft. I stood outside for a minute looking up through the ancient trees into my grainy and discouraging future, my back and shoulder muscles fizzing and burning like dynamite fuses from carrying my bags three miles. A wrought-iron hoot owl stared down at me from the third floor. I did not want to stay here. Neither did I want to walk another three miles carrying these bags to end up in similar quarters for the indigent.

The landlady poked her head out the door. 'Are you the one who called?'

When you land in the new place, never waste your energy trying to convince a stranger you're honest. Only liars can do this effectively. My landlady didn't trust me. Who knows how many rapists, con artists, and serial murderers entered her living room nightly via the television set? And the general record of people applying to live in rooming houses did nothing to recommend me either. But money is more powerful than fear, and she was not running this rooming house for the love of mankind, so after I forked over the bulk of my estate, she led me up the stairs to my new home: a clean little room with a chair, a bed, a radiator, a dresser, and a desk.

It rained for the first sixty days I was in Fond du Lac. No, that isn't true. Occasionally it snowed. After two days in which I did not rape, con, or murder anyone, my landlady decided I was all right, and, in a sudden shower of generosity, supplied me with long-sleeved shirts, slippers, two television sets (which I never used), ashtrays, a home-cooked meatloaf dinner, and blankets and black sheets for the bed. I lay on my black sheets (black sheets, have you any wool?) while it rained or snowed outside and for the most part, because of my neck and the ache in my left arm, I did not sleep. When I did sleep it was only ten- or twenty-minute snatches in contorted Gumby postures, chin tucked down onto chest or arms arranged in an octopus pile over my head.

My housemates all had alcohol problems. Who else would live in a room without even a sink, share a refrigerator and a bathroom with four strangers, and give up almost complete privacy while the fruit flies spin in a galactic heap above the meaty-fumed trash that no one ever takes out? My neighbors were Bobbie, a head-injury case; Ginny, a bartender who had just finished an alcohol treatment program but had begun to drink again 'now and then' (see ya later, couch potater); Jess in the basement, who had once been a Lutheran minister but was now a full-time drunk; and Dave, who had never been anything as far as I could tell except perhaps a child before he had become a drunk. Dave serenaded me nightly around 2 a.m. after the bars had closed, sloshing about in the gravel below as he

struggled to secure his bicycle: *Fucking sons of bitches!*
Fuckin' A! I don't give a shit where you go with that son of a
bitch now. . .!

Drunks are at heart antisocial, and I was grateful to be
left alone by all of my housemates, except for Bobbie, the
head-injury case, who attached herself to me almost
immediately. An unemployed, forty-six-year-old Clairol
redhead, Bobbie had suffered two head injuries, first when
she fell off the back of a motorcycle somewhere in the pan-
handle of Oklahoma, and then when she got mugged by a
madman with a tire iron at a mall in Minnesota. The second
attack required surgery, facial reconstruction. Epilepsy also
came with the second attack and the damage to her brain.

While I knew her, Bobbie spent as many as sixteen hours
a day in front of the television, and even when she climbed
out of bed for a beer, she never left her impenetrable fog
of TV fantasy. As soon as she learned I planned to return
to Mexico in six months, my name became 'Gringo,' and
she decided we were going to travel together to L.A., where
she had lived for seven years. Bobbie dreamed of her old
life in L.A., camping on the beach in Malibu, driving with
the top down on the movie-star freeways, having a great
job as a computer programmer. She stole whatever she liked
from the refrigerator — especially my beer — and trapped
people against the wall and talked them to death. Each time
I began to prepare a meal in the community kitchen, she
broke away from her television program to follow me
around and stick her nose into my pots: 'Mmmm. So you

cook the vegetables right into it? You'll have to give me the recipe. You make your own SALAD dressing? What do you put in it? Can I have a glass of that wine? What kind of wine is it? Oh, CHEAP wine, that sounds nice. Just fill it right to the top there...'

THE RENT ALWAYS COMES DUE FASTER WHEN YOU DON'T HAVE a job, and I had about a hundred dollars left and this idea that I was going to save up three grand in six months and leave Wisconsin before the first big snow, so I got busy right away looking through the paper at the jobs no one else wanted: short-order cook, housekeeping, roofing, convenience-store clerk, hospital assistant. Every day there are more restaurants, more motels, more convenience stores, more hospitals, and they all have roofs, creating more and more jobs that nobody wants. 'Join a winning team!' 'Are you a self-motivated go-getting ignoramus who works well with others?' 'Need extra cash for spinal-cord surgery?' For days, I followed up these ads. I registered at the state-run Job Service, which was entirely computerized, so you never had to deal with a human being unless one of the printers jammed. One day I walked to North Fond du Lac, a sixteen-mile round trip, where a cooking job was listed through Job Service at twelve dollars an hour.

'Oh, by the way,' said the owner, after I'd filled out the application, 'that wage listing at Job Service is not right. I don't know why they keep putting in twelve dollars an hour. It's eight dollars an hour.'

I walked the eight miles home. No sidewalks along the highway. The people yelled at me from their cars. 'Blow me!' 'Waaaaah!'

The next day, walking home from the post office, I saw a sign in a window advertising factory jobs. I went in and filled out an hour's worth of forms. They photocopied my Social Security card and Kansas driver's license. I filled out a W-4. I solved arithmetic problems. I didn't even know what I was applying for.

Finally, I was 'interviewed' in the back room. Oh, an employment service. They take a cut from your wage, don't they? No, they cover your insurance and the employer pays them above the base wage. This is cheaper than having to pay employees sick leave, vacation, pension fund, medical insurance, etc. They can fire you any time they like, owe you nothing, not a minute's notice, not a good-luck trinket or a handshake goodbye. This is America the machine. It works quite well. The people in the machine look a little dazed, however. They have dyed their hair purple. They are covered with jewelry and tattoos. Their children are scattered across the country. They have serious substance-abuse problems. They are working on a historically unparalleled suicide rate. They exhibit about as much joy and innocence as old whores out on the boulevard. But the machine is working very smoothly, thank you.

The good thing about working for temporary services is that you don't have to lie to your employer: 'Yes, I plan to stay to the end of my life in your toaster-part factory.' With a temp service the relationship is purely mercenary. Neither of us is on a winning team. All hail to the machine.

Darlene, my temp rep, wore a short skirt and showed me her cleavage. Add Darlene to the list of things I like about America. I think many people like temp services because they get to deal with the cleavage — I mean to say, the human. The new computerized state employment systems are very effective. I had no breakdowns and everything printed up well and all the addresses were right, but it was a lonesome experience. Looking for jobs is no fun, and it's nice to have some cleavage — I mean to say, some encouragement, or what appears to be guidance or sympathy — as you blunder about being turned down by one place after the next.

Looking for jobs is no fun, but what is less fun is actually getting the job. I am usually sent to either wood shop or metal shop, two of my weakest areas. In this case Darlene lined me up with a wood shop called the North American Container Corporation, a warehouse two and a half miles away that should've been called Shoot-Out at the OK Corral. The shop floor sounded like this: BLAM! BLAM! BLAM! BLAM! BLAM! BLAM! BLAM! BLAM! — thirty people with nail and staple guns whirling around jigs (metal tables) nailing together pallets (wooden platforms upon which cargo is stacked) as fast as they could go. Seven twenty-five an hour. Someone handed me a nail gun with sixteen seconds of instruction (don't shoot yourself in the hand) and off I went. BLAM! BLAM! BLAM! BLAM! BLAM! BLAM! BLAM! BLAM!

On my third day working at the pallet factory, my hand frozen in a numb claw from firing that nail gun, I stopped for a moment to investigate a sudden sensation of cool air in my briefs and found that my jeans were shredded across the thighs. Then I noticed that my shoelace had broken, and my 'work' gloves, which I'd bought two days before at the drugstore, had two holes in them. These were my only pants, my only shoes, my only gloves. It was pouring outside. Lightning throbbed in eerie violet streaks against the sky. But I had to work the next day, so I had no choice but to walk to the store that night in the rain and buy a new pair of pants, gloves, and shoelaces.

When the three-thirty buzzer sounded, I clocked out and headed through the rain for the mall and Sears, which, according to my antique perception of the world, was the only place to get everything work-related you needed. It was at least three miles to the mall. I had to stop and ask twice for directions. I was glad that it was raining because all the people who would normally shout at me from their cars had their big mouths on the other side of their rolled-up windows.

Every American city, even one you have never been to before, becomes familiar as you get close to the freeway and Taco Bell and the rest of it. Walking around now in America is like walking around inside of a television set. The Applebee's in Bangor isn't any different from the one in Pahrump. Ditto Wal-Mart. Weather is about the only tangible distinction between cities anymore, which is why people continue to flock to overcrowded places like Florida and California. Warm weather with Wal-Mart and Applebee's.

Sears was a disappointment. I found a small pile of work pants and two styles of gloves to choose from, 'light gardening' and 'tea party.' The work pants, twenty-dollar Roebucks, had a two-year guarantee. In the dressing room sawdust was falling out of my wrecked old jeans and my back was so stiff I couldn't bend over to take off my shoes. The laughter burst songlike from my throat. I like to think I can appreciate a good joke, even if it is on me.

The saleslady poked her head into the dressing room. 'Everything all right?' 'Sorry,' I said, 'just my ridiculous life.'

I also bought a pair of forty-five-inch 'work' shoelaces at Sears, which turned out to mean that you had to 'work' to keep them tied. Dapper in my new Roebucks and fresh laces that came untied every five minutes, I left the mall. The wind snapped up, blowing off my cap, and it began to rain in earnest. The K-Mart across the street had an excellent selection of work gloves, and I finally settled on a pair of Wells Lamont Professional Jersey Hob-Nobs (sewn in Jamaica of American-made materials) for $2.99; seven-day gloves if I ever saw them.

It was six o'clock now. I wouldn't get home until at least seven. By the time I showered, shaved, cooked dinner, and packed a lunch for the next day, it would be time to go to bed. I thought about Bobbie appearing the moment I lit a burner on the stove. A Kentucky Fried Chicken, the answer to all my uniquely American problems, shimmered in the distance.

'I would like some chicken,' I told the teenage girl at the counter. 'Just chicken. No dinner packages, value meals, curly fries, *Star Wars* figures, or anything like that.' I had not had KFC chicken in recent memory and thought this clever à-la-carte strategy would save me some money.

'Would you like eight, twelve, or sixteen pieces?' she said.

'Give me twelve,' I said.

'Thirteen ninety-nine,' she said.

'Thirteen ninety-nine,' I replied dumbly, looking into my wallet.

'I'm not going to give you any wings,' said the elderly woman tonging my pieces into a box. 'It's not every day that I do that.'

'I appreciate that,' I said, thankful that I had enough money left to buy beer.

It was colder than ever when I left the KFC, but the rain had stopped. I was hungry, and as I walked along I dragged a thigh out of the box. This chicken was hotter than a volcano. I fumbled with it, swearing, and finally got it out into the cold air, where I could eat it, snorting and wincing. That KFC is good chicken. I'm not going to add it to the list of things I like about America, though, because it is more than a dollar a piece. I could've bought four whole chickens for thirteen ninety-nine.

Along the way, I stopped at the drugstore and spent the last of my money on two twenty-four-ounce beers. It was almost dark. Turning down my street, I heard two little girls riding their bicycles behind me. They were chirping delightfully in their happy little voices. Then came a big crash. I turned around to find the little girl in the pink jacket sprawled over her fallen bike, crying, her training wheels still spinning. I walked back, set my bags down on the lawn, and helped her up. Frightened and hurt, she threw her arms around my neck and held me, bawling and bawling. I tried to console her. She was not hurt badly, maybe a little bruised, but mostly scared. I remembered how scary it was falling off my bike, especially the first time, so I talked to her about falling off my bike. Then I kissed the tips of my fingers and touched them to her forehead and told her that I loved her.

She stepped back and stopped crying for a second as if to comprehend this odd stranger. Then the tears started up again, and the big brother arrived, freckle-faced and severe, more concerned about me, I think, than his sister. He'd read about abducted children on the sides of milk cartons. I'd forgotten where I was for a moment. In America, a stranger does not touch children or tell them he loves them. (In Mexico I probably would've been invited in for dinner.)

I tied my work laces, picked up my chicken and beer, and abandoned the scene. For a while, the child's sweetness and wet little green eyes stayed with me.

ONE OF MY TRICKS FOR KEEPING AN UNDESIRABLE JOB IS TO tell myself I am quitting on Friday. I won't quit on Friday, but the thought of it keeps me going. 'Well, just two more days and I am out of this rotten place,' I tell myself. 'One more day and I am gone, daddy, gone.' And then, once I make it to the weekend and have the pay-check in pocket and a couple of days to rest up and read books on my black-sheeted bed while the rain sifts and spatters against the screen, I say to myself, 'All right then, maybe just one more week, but on Friday...'

I went through three pairs of Wells Lamont Professional Jersey Hob-Nobs before all the temporary people at the pallet factory were suddenly laid off. No notice. I was mostly relieved.

That afternoon, I went to see Darlene, who freshened my spirits with her cleavage.

'How would you like to make $8.60 an hour?' she said.

'What kind of job is it?'

'Sheet-metal house.'

'Metal shop,' I said.

'All shifts available,' she said.

'And for good reason,' I added.

'It'll keep you out of trouble,' she said with a wink, handing me my assignment card.

All I had to do was march back out that night to the mall to buy steel-toed shoes.

The difference between the pallet factory and the sheet-metal house can be summarized as follows: BLAM! BLAM! BLAM! BLAM! versus KA-WHUMP! KA-WHUMP! KA-WHUMP! KA-WHUMP! The sheet-metal house is actually louder: a dozen giant hydraulic presses smashing out a stamped metal part every three to thirty seconds and shaking the earth like a stampede of *T. rex* coming after your picnic basket, plus the whir of leviathan flywheels and fans to keep the grit moving through the air and the oldies or country station blaring ineffectively over the top of the whole racket. The sheet-metal house pays a little better because people are always being rushed off to the hospital. Besides the obvious crushing power of the machines, the sheet metal is thin and sharp, and when you work with literally tons of it every day, you get cut. A kid I worked with got sliced straight through his glove, eighteen stitches. Another woman there got taken out one night on a stretcher. I asked one of the third-shift operators when he was taking over my machine one night how long he'd been there and he held up three stubs for fingers. Sometimes you are working with very small parts and you can't wear gloves. One day I brought a meatball sandwich with ketchup on it and when I stopped for dinner I had so many bleeding cuts on my fingers I could not tell the difference between me and the sauce.

WHEN THE WISCONSIN WEATHER WARMS, THE HUMIDITY GETS SO thick as you move through it that the catfish nibble at your ankles and you can turn around at any moment and see the exact shape of your body cut in a tunnel through the mist. I could not breathe in that humidity. None of the over-the-counter asthma medications, epinephrine and ephedrine, worked for me. My father, an asthmatic, sent me Albuterol, which didn't work either. I quit smoking, but that didn't help.

Then the insects began to appear—especially the famous jumbo mosquitoes, which are so big they sag as they fly.

Wisconsin mosquitoes are larger than average mosquitoes because they carry extra blood-sucking equipment and amplifying devices to announce in your ears that they have arrived as you try to sleep broken-necked and wheezing at four o'clock in the morning. Mexican and tropical mosquitoes are almost impossible to kill without flamethrowers. However, Wisconsin mosquitoes are easy to kill because they are so much larger and slower and apparently stupid and complacent from their worldwide reputations, like free-agent baseball players. Never mind, insect success is based upon large numbers. You can kill one or two or perhaps eighteen sagging jumbo mosquitoes, but beyond that you must say to yourself: 'I am moving from this place very soon.'

I have always had an inclination toward despair. Combine this with living in a culture where money, actuarial tables, and TV-watching are the primary human bonds; being unable to sleep or breathe; having a lousy job; Bobbie stealing my food and beer; everyone around me dressed up like pirates, bikers, gangsters, or ghouls; and giant mosquitoes swarming through the cracks clutching knives and forks polished brightly by the dinner napkins tied around their necks, and you have the formula for depression. Uncle Wiggly, my friend in the pharmaceutical business, who prizes my ability to remain lost but regularly fears that I will do myself in, sent me a bottle of Prozac. I got the package on Friday and started taking the pills immediately.

I know many people who swear by various antidepressants, but the Prozac didn't work for me. (I was still the same person in the same place with the same job, wasn't I?) All it did was fill my head with wool. On my best day, I felt like a bucket of coleslaw. Uncle Wiggly assured me it would take some time to adjust as the fluoxotene built up in my system. I didn't like the sound of this. I am a nomenologist, a believer that the names of things are an indication of their true natures, and 'Prozac' sounds to me like an iron planet inhabited solely by androids.

About this time, I talked to my friend Sara, who was tending bar in North Carolina while waiting for grad school to start. Sara was excited when I told her I'd come to live in the land of her favorite young adult romance, and it was principally because of her that I was there. In other words, it was all her fault. I warned her that Fond du Lac would be a disappointment. She said she couldn't expect anything to live up to the image of *Seventeenth Summer*. I said it might be a little worse than that, but it would be wonderful to see her. The place could use a little sunshine.

Sara stayed at the Ramada Inn, which I listed before at $70 a night, but was actually $120 a night, blow dryer, ironing board, coffeemaker, twenty-four-inch cable TV, basketful of exotic toiletries. Someone had written in ink on the door where the rates and rules were posted: 'This is too high, isn't it?' But Sara only paid $60, some sort of special attractive-young-bartender rate. I suppose if the room is listed at $120 a night, and you pay only $60, you feel like you're getting a deal.

Sara is smart, dark-haired, dark-eyed, and very well

developed. It was dangerous to walk along the road with her because the imitation bikers swerved closer in their rusted Pontiacs to shout at her from their windows.

'Nice tits!' yelled a young trick-or-treater wearing a goatee and a gold-loop earring.

'Thank you!' I called back, thrusting out my chest proudly.

SARA HADN'T SLEPT FOR A COUPLE OF DAYS AND I HADN'T SLEPT for a couple of months, but we didn't sleep at all for the two days she was there. Never mind if I was impotent. Sara was starved to talk about ideas and books and didn't seem to mind if I was a eunuch, although if you are a eunuch and entertaining a beautiful woman who has just traveled two thousand miles to see you, the conversation better be good. I kept taking secret little blasts of Albuterol, because if you can't breathe *or* make love someone might drive you against your will to a mortuary.

'I don't know what it is,' I confessed. 'Can I blame it on the Prozac?'

She thought for a full minute before she finally said: 'It must be difficult to be a man.'

'I'm glad you didn't use the word "hard",' I said.

That night we took a long walk through town. There are more bars per capita in Fond du Lac than in any other city I have ever encountered, including Tijuana and the alcoholic outposts of the rainy northwest. The bars were letting out and the Fond du Lackers were in fine fettle. We listened to a gaggle of drunken children who could not formulate a sentence without the word *fuck*. Bottles were shattered all along the sidewalk. A pay phone had been vandalized, the broken receiver hanging from a fray of colored wires. Sara stopped in her tracks. The word DEAD was spelled in blue spray paint below her feet. 'Why don't you get out of here?' she asked me.

'Because if I left now it would take all the money I have saved to start all over again.'

After Sara left I stopped taking the Prozac, although Uncle Wiggly urged me to continue the regimen. I suppose it's important that you believe in a treatment for it to work. Well, I believe that Prozac works; I just don't believe that a neurochemical imbalance is the cause of my depression. There are plenty of good reasons to be depressed in America without blaming it on neurotransmitters.

OFTEN, WHEN BOBBIE DRANK, HER DREAM OF TRAVELING WITH me across the country blossomed, and she would knock on my door calling my name until I answered. One afternoon she knocked while I was taking a nap. I sat up blearily in bed, not in the mood for another daydreaming session. 'What is it?'

'Can you help me, Gringo? I'm having a seizure.'

Bobbie had no one in her life but her mother and her social workers. I pulled on my pants and opened the door. She stood before me hunched and shivering, eyes rolled up into her head like the reels in a busted slot machine. Bobbie would often feign illnesses to get what she wanted (the state had recently assigned her a housekeeper because she claimed she couldn't make her bed), but she was not making this one up.

'What do you want me to do?' I said.

'Just sit with me,' she said. 'My mother is on the way.'

We sat on the couch in the parlor. I was not familiar with her type of epilepsy. She didn't flop or convulse or vomit. She only shivered, her eyes disarranged spookily, her speech chopped and slurred.

'Rub my arms,' she said.

I rubbed her forearms and kept her in the conscious realm by getting her to talk about her diet book. Bobbie was about twenty pounds overweight and ate mainly frozen meals from the microwave, breakfast cereal, and whatever else I had picked up from the grocery store, but she was gung-ho on a diet she had developed long ago in L.A. 'It's a surefire diet,' she slurred. 'But I am not going to refund people's money.'

'You have to guarantee your diet,' I said. 'Besides, when people go on a diet and it doesn't work, they are just ashamed of themselves. They never ask for a refund.'

'I have lost up to forty pounds on this diet,' she added. 'Fast.'

'I have a good diet too,' I said. 'It's the asthmatic, walk-five-miles-a-day, lousy-job, live-alone, sleep-poorly, and smoke-anyway diet. I have lost twenty-five pounds since I left Mexico.'

Bobbie laughed. 'I'm going to get a cigarette,' she said.

'Stay here, Gringo. Don't go away.' She staggered up and teetered off, listing to one side like a ship in heavy seas.

'I'm not supposed to smoke when I'm having a seizure,' she explained, returning with the cigarette, 'but the hell with it. Will you light it for me?'

Bobbie smoked GPCS, which are manufactured by the Goodyear Tire and Rubber Company, shredding-and-rolling division.

'The drinking doesn't help either,' I added.

'Don't talk about drinking in front of my mother.'

'It's your life,' I said.

'I don't drink that much, anyway.'

'How long do these seizures usually last?' I asked.

'Sometimes as long as twelve hours.'

I'd never heard of twelve-hour epileptic seizures before, but then I know very little about most things and less than nothing about the rest. Her mother, a short spunky woman in running shoes, finally arrived. It was hard to imagine the two being related, though I knew that Bobbie had been in all phases of her existence violently altered by fate. I wondered for the thousandth time what she had been like before, and what the change meant: if our lives are random tragedies or carefully designed sequences of bad luck.

Bobbie's eyes had dropped back into place. The shivering had stopped.

'I'm going to go now,' I said.

'Thank you so much for staying with me, Gringo,' she said.

JULY WAS A MONTH THAT SEEMED TO LAST FOR SEVERAL YEARS. One day at work I stooped to retrieve this pile of liner paper that was spilling out of a moving three-ton coil of stainless steel, and my head collided with the outstretched piece of sheet metal, sending my hat and safety glasses flying. I clamped my gloved hand to my forehead and staggered around a bit waiting for the pain to go away. Two mechanics stood in front of me, looking urgent and condescending. 'You OK, buddy? You OK?'

'Sure, fine,' I said. 'Just bumped my head.' I took my hand away to show them.

Head wounds tend to bleed a lot. This one was no exception. My left glove was already soaked. I switched to the other. 'Why don't you go to first-aid?' the mechanics suggested. 'We'll find your supervisor for you.'

In the first-aid room, a crowd of semimedical experts nervously swarmed around me. I even had the attention of two of the big cheeses, probably for insurance purposes. When my supervisor saw the gash, she almost fainted. I might as well have jumped face first into a kitchen knife.

'It's a good one,' everyone kept telling me. Well, I am no metal-shop genius, so I was glad to hear that I had at last done something good.

'Looks like about twelve stitches,' said Don, the top first-aid expert. Don and I were the only ones who seemed relaxed: he, because he saw people mangled and cut up all day; I, because I just felt stupid and lost in the long defeat of another job I wasn't very good at.

Don wrapped my head up turban-style and gave me a ride

to the emergency room, where a nice nurse cleaned me up and prepared me for the needle. Then I lay on that crisp tissue-paper-covered emergency-room bed holding back the blood for two hours. More urgent cases kept coming in: a bad bicycle wreck, a motorcycle accident (which turned out to be a fatality), a retired fellow who'd gotten run over by his own riding mower. He was in the bed next to mine, behind the curtain, and kept saying over and over, 'I must have put it in gear with my foot. I just changed the oil and I was going to take it for a ride...' He had tire tracks across his chest and had nearly lost an arm. Somewhere, a baby kept crying, and I felt so witless and sad just lying there. *Oh, you little baby*, I thought, *I will give up my dumb life for you, just please stop crying.*

Finally, a doctor showed up, asked me a few cursory questions — all the while nodding as if it were perfectly natural to walk into a stretched-out piece of sheet metal — covered my face with one of those tissue-paper toilet-seat covers, spiked me with a topical, and began to pluck away with the catgut. 'It's a good one,' he said. 'Oh, yes.' Knit one, purl two. He swore a little under his breath. The blood poured like a Haydn Concerto down the sides of my face and into my ears.

'How you doing down there?'

'Pretty good, how is everything up there?'

And the baby cried and the man next to me having his arm sewn back on said for the sixteenth time: 'I must have put it in gear with my foot...'

NOT LONG AFTER THAT, THE METAL-SHOP SUPERVISOR, Jan (pronounced 'Yawn,' apparently a nickname given to him by his wife), came up to me and said, 'We'd like to hire you' — which goes to show you how desperate employers are to fill spots in front of these hydraulic maiming machines. He was a hairy-necked gorilla of a man built in a muscular wedge all the way down to tiny dancer's feet.

'I'd love to stay,' I said, being polite, 'but I'm leaving soon.'

'You're leaving?' he said, raising his eyebrows. 'When?'

'I don't know exactly. Maybe a month.'

'Where you going?'

'Mexico. That's where I came from.'

He hemmed a bit. 'Well, let us know when you're leaving.' He turned off nimbly and lumbered away.

The next day, a woman I'd never seen before came up to me, tilting her head into my face like a smooth-faced rodent, and said, 'I'm sorry, but this will be your last day here. We tried to call you but you couldn't be reached. We actually had you off the list but since you came in today we'll let you work to the end of the shift. We're sorry. We wanted to hire you.'

I felt sick and dull and betrayed, the way you always feel when someone has let you go, even if it's a dreadful job. If I would've lied to Yawn about my intention to stay, I could've spared myself the trouble of looking for another job.

'HAVE YOU EVER THOUGHT ABOUT WORKING IN A CHEESE factory?' Darlene asked me as she leaned forward and tapped a few keys on her computer.

'To be honest with you, I have never considered it,' I answered. I immediately liked the idea, though. For one thing, a cheese factory wasn't wood or metal shop. And it was a little piece of Wisconsin to take with me, like a Hawaiian postcard with a photo of a Hilton Inn on it.

'Do I need steel-toed boots?' I said. 'Safety glasses? Earplugs? A first-aid kit?'

'No,' she said, handing me my assignment with a weary and sympathetic grin. 'But you might want to bring a clothespin.'

The wood shop goes BLAM! BLAM! BLAM! BLAM! BLAM! BLAM! BLAM! BLAM! and the metal shop goes KA-WHUMP! KA-WHUMP! KA-WHUMP! KA-WHUMP! and the cheese factory goes: MY! WHAT IS THAT AROMA? The shifts were nine hours long, eight dollars an hour. The employees, mostly women, were dressed in androgynous white lab outfits and disposable paper hairnets that made them look like extras in a Dutch remake of *The Andromeda Strain*. On my first day I started out running three-pound wheels of blue cheese through a metal detector, then bagging and boxing them. Later, I was transferred to a room where cosmetically rejected wheels (usually too moldy) of blue cheese were being crumbled and bagged for restaurant sales. I stood and heaped three- to ten-pound wheels of cheese onto an inclined conveyor belt, then sprinkled them with a white powder that I thought was flour.

'No, it's a preservative,' the girl next to me said.

'Good thing,' I said. 'We wouldn't want this stuff to mold.'

Cheese work is very easy. The rooms are cool. There's no one bleeding, or losing fingers, or shooting nails into their hands. You can hear the music on the radio. But the mold and the damp fetidness and the fine, floury haze of preservatives compounded my already chronic bronchial problems. Toward the end of the shift, as my blood-oxygen level sank, the hands on the clock began to jump forward and back, like children playing 'Red Light, Green Light.' How embarrassing it is to suffocate on your first day at work! I fled the cheese factory the moment the clock struck eleven. It was a sticky night, the humidity off the scale. I toiled the two miles home through an atmosphere so soggy I could not hear the pinging of submarines over my own labored breathing.

When I got to the rooming house, the door to Bobbie's room was open, and she was lying on her bed, cackling at a Whoopi Goldberg movie, a bottle of my Heineken in her hand. A package from Uncle Wiggly had arrived. I tore it open. Inside were two aerosol inhalers, *Flovent* and *Serevent*. 'One puff of each at morning and night,' the note read. 'Efficacy guaranteed.' I took a full blast of each, fairly certain that these miracle asthma medications could not help me. In minutes, however, I was breathing freely. Grateful and amazed, I poured myself a glass of wine and sat down to update my list:

9. *Inhaled corticosteroids.*
10. *Uncle Wiggly.*

Bobbie began knocking on my door. 'Gringo, are you in there?'

11. *The first big snow in Wisconsin.*

'Gringo, are you home?'

12. *A Greyhound bus headed for the Mexican border.*

Estrellita

THE RAINY SEASON HAD BEGUN A MONTH BEFORE. IT USUALLY rained at night, sometimes all night. I lived in a large empty house above a bus station, one of two terminals in Jerez, a quiet Mexican town of sixty thousand. The evenings were peaceful but a bit too long. From my dim, unfurnished living room, I would watch the rain slide in a slanted sheet from the rooftop. It was like living behind a waterfall.

One night, feeling restless after two or three drinks, I decided to visit my friend Ismael the woodcarver, who lived three blocks away. It was about nine o'clock. The rain had just stopped. As I closed my front door and began to walk up the street, someone called to me. I turned and saw a young girl approach out of the darkness. She appeared neat and studentlike, slightly stooped by the weight of a backpack, a brand-new notebook under her arm. Her long, shiny hair was pulled back into a ponytail. She spoke to me in rapid Spanish, in a pipsqueak voice.

'Do you speak any English?' I asked.

'No.'

'You must speak more slowly then,' I told her in Spanish.

'Can you tell me where the bus station is?' she said.

'Yes, it's right there,' I said, pointing to the closed steel gate. Normally, the gate would have been up and a crowd would've been gathered by the big planter out front, waiting for the next bus. But tonight the area around the planter was vacant.

'Usually the terminal is open until ten,' I explained.

She looked up at me with concern. She had pale greenish eyes, a long neck, and little gaps between her teeth. She shifted the weight on her back.

'Are there any more buses?' she asked me.

'I don't know,' I said.

She showed me a blue twenty-peso note. 'Do you know where else I can buy a ticket?'

'Maybe from the…' I mimed holding a steering wheel, unable to think of the Spanish word for *driver*.

'But what if there is not another bus?' she asked.

'Where do you live?' I said.

'Arroyo Seco.'

I recognized the name of a little rancho to the south. 'How far is it?'

She pressed a finger to her lips, tilting her head. 'About nine kilometers.'

Too far for a young girl to walk in the dark along the narrow road, I thought, even though she probably would've been safe. I rang the doorbell of Angel, who ran the bus station. There was no answer. Both of his cars were gone, and all the lights in his house were off.

'Sometimes he takes his family to Puerto Vallarta,' I said. 'He might not be back for three days.'

'What am I going to do?' she said. 'How am I going to get to Arroyo Seco?'

I shrugged. 'If I had a car, I would give you a ride.'

'Are you a *gringo*?' she said, peering up at me with a slight, playful smile.

No one in this town had ever mistaken me for anything else. I was also called 'white boy' and '*guerro*.'

'Yes,' I said.

'Will you give me something to eat?' she said.

I wasn't sure if I had understood her correctly. She didn't seem poor and had none of the mannerisms of a hustler.

'What are you doing in Jerez?' I said.

'I've been going to school.'

'It seems a little late for school.'

'I was at a friend's house,' she said.

I asked if she might be able to spend the night with her friend. She said that wouldn't be possible.

'Isn't there anyone you can call?'

'Oh, no,' she said, making her eyes big.

'I don't know what I can do to help you,' I said.

'Can I stay the night with you?'

Again, I wondered if I had heard right. I scratched my head, then asked if she wanted to come with me to the house of my friend Don Ismael, who spoke both English and Spanish and knew much more about Jerez than I. Perhaps he would be able to help her. She eagerly agreed, and I let her put her notebook and backpack inside my locked door for safekeeping.

'I'm thirteen years old,' she announced as we crossed the street.

She looked older than thirteen. Fifteen maybe. I told her I was forty-four, old enough to be her father. *More* than old enough. She laughed and then began to cough. It was not a phony cough.

'Are you sick?' I said.

'A little.'

We crossed the bridge over the river, which was usually stagnant or dry, but now ran swiftly from a month of good rains. She seemed happy just to tag along with me wherever I went. I didn't know if this was an indication of trust or innocence or desperation. Perhaps I should've been the one who was worried.

'Where are your parents?' I said.

'I have no parents.'

'Do you have any grandparents?'

'No.'

'Brothers or sisters?'

'No.'

'Aunts or uncles?'

'No.'

'You have no family?'

'I have no one,' she replied cheerfully, swinging her arms and looking up at the sky. 'And I would like something to eat.'

We turned the corner onto Enrique Estrada, Ismael's street, where Arnufo the taco vendor was stationed under the blue tarp of his outdoor stand. Arnufo was about thirty and had two small children, who could usually be found scrambling over the cases of soda pop. He pulled a piece of sizzling meat out of the boiling lard, flopped it onto a tree stump, and began to whack away at it with a hatchet.

'*Buenas noches*, Arnufo,' I said as we passed, wondering what he thought of my walking the streets at this time of night with a strange young girl.

Arnufo nodded to me. If he thought anything he didn't show it.

The little girl glanced at the meat and smiled. 'It smells good.'

'What's your name?' I said, realizing I hadn't asked.

'Estrellita,' she said.

LIKE MANY PEOPLE IN THIS PART OF MEXICO, ISMAEL LIVED IN a cement building in a walled-in lot behind a great steel door. I knocked and shouted his name, but there was no response. He lived far back in the corner of his property, in a little two-room dwelling. Perhaps he couldn't hear us. *She will have to spend the night with me*, I thought. How is it that I had become this child's guardian in a matter of minutes? I had no children and never wanted any. I was not up to the task.

I stood for a minute longer, looking up at Ismael's aqua-colored door.

'Should we try again?' Estrellita asked.

I knocked once more, then realized the door was unlocked. Ismael often left it open, even late at night, so he wouldn't miss visitors. We went in.

Off to the left was Ismael's workshop, covered only by a corrugated iron roof. A light glowed dimly in the house. He was home. *Good*, I thought. *Maybe he will be in the mood for adoption.* The girl followed me closely. '*Puercos,*' I said, as we passed a small cement stall that held two smelly black pigs, which Ismael was raising for slaughter. Estrellita giggled.

Through the window, I could see Ismael working at his computer. He was sixty-nine, knobby and twisted like an old troll from thirty years of felling trees in the forests of Oregon and Washington. What was left of his hair hung in soft snow-white curls to his shoulders. His coarse, severely neat white mustache was yellow at the edge from nicotine.

Ismael jumped up when he heard my voice. I don't know who he thought the girl was, but when he saw her, he brightened even more and turned on all the lights to show off his museum of woodworking treasures. Around the kitchen were carved figures, sculpted picture frames, finely wrought panels and plaques, and a hope chest in progress. Drawings for a de'Medici bed frame were spread across his drafting table. Ismael was a fine carver, famous in the Pacific Northwest in his day.

I pointed to my little friend. 'This is Estrellita.' I said. 'She has a problem.'

Ismael's face fell. 'What's the problem?' he said.

'She lives in Arroyo Seco'—Ismael had been born and raised not far from there—'and she's stranded in Jerez. She says she has no family. Tell him the story,' I said to Estrellita.

Ismael gestured us into the bedroom and sat down in front of his computer, which he'd just hooked up the day before.

As my little charge stood before Ismael and recited her tale, he began to look doubtful. Again, she seemed happy just to be around people who might tell her what to do. Perhaps the warm house and the presence of adults reassured her. If she was entirely on her own at age thirteen, this would only be natural. I asked Ismael to inquire about her family. I didn't catch her reply, but he suddenly appeared to be fed up with her. She glanced back and forth between us. The sweet and gratefully optimistic look in her eyes reminded me of a stray dog who'd been taken in for the night. I think she would've been content just to stay with us, perhaps for several years.

Ismael told Estrellita he was certain that another bus, one that would stop at Arroyo Seco, would be coming along soon. It would be the last bus south for the night. She would be able to buy her ticket from the driver. Twenty pesos would be plenty. He told her she should hurry if she wanted to catch that last bus.

'I'll take her back to the station,' I said.

'Are you coming back?' Ismael asked me.

'As soon as I get her squared away.'

'Good.' He lit a Mexican Marlboro and returned to his computer.

Estrellita and I walked back out through the darkness, past the dark, sad smell of the *puercos*. She trotted along fearlessly and obediently behind me. As we exited by the great metal door, she reminded me that she was hungry.

We stopped at Arnufo's little taco stand. Arnufo was always working to support his growing family. During the day, when he could not find cement-laying work for seven pesos an hour, he shined shoes in the plaza. Every evening at sundown, rain or shine, he set up his taco stand. I ordered three *tacos adobada* (pork) to go. Estrellita looked up at me sweetly and asked for a *refresco*. What kind? Strawberry. She gave me those big eyes, and I rolled mine a little, but I didn't mind. The whole meal cost not much more than a dollar, bottle deposit included.

As we walked back to the bus station, Estrellita was bubbly and full of questions. She wanted to know where I was from, what I did for a living, why I wanted to live in Jerez, why I didn't have a wife and children. Two men were sitting on the planter waiting for the bus when we arrived. As Ismael predicted, another bus was due, and it would stop in Arroyo Seco. I got Estrellita's things out from behind my door. She took her place at the planter, foil-wrapped tacos in one hand, strawberry pop in the other, the most contented-looking stranded child I have ever seen. I asked the men to look after her.

'*Gracias*!' she called to me in her pipsqueak voice as I walked away.

When I returned to Ismael's house, he poured me a glass of Xalixco tequila, which he liked to mix with orange soda, and we talked about the girl. He shook his head. He didn't believe her stories.

I told him I thought she made an unlikely hustler. There had to be some truth in what she had said. On any other night, she would've been successful in her original intention of catching a bus. Only because the station was closed had she been forced to rely on me.

Ismael remained skeptical. 'She wanted something from you,' he said, 'and she got it, didn't she?'

'A few tacos,' I said.

'You're a soft touch.'

'I prefer to think of it as kindness from a stranger.'

'Kindness from a sucker is more like it,' Ismael said.

'How can you be sure she wasn't on her own?'

He scoffed. 'Arroyo Seco is a small town,' he said. 'A thirteen-year-old child would not live alone.'

Outside, it began to rain hard: chattering, slashing, jungle rain. I wondered whether Estrellita had caught her bus or whether she was stuck out in the rain with her soggy tacos and bottle of strawberry pop. Did she have enough money for a ticket? And who, if anyone, would be waiting for her when she got home?

Ismael and I played pinochle on his new computer while lightning crashed in ghastly green sheets against the curtains and thunder cracked and rumbled like an avalanche of bowling balls. Afraid of a power surge, we shut off the computer, then drank a good half-liter of tequila mixed with a liter of Fanta orange, smoked a dozen cigarettes, and each ate four tacos, which I bought from Arnufo's stand in the rain. At 1 a.m. I had to leave, rain or no. Ismael loaned me his rain jacket and straw hat.

On the way home in the steady downpour, I continued to think of Estrellita. Even if she wasn't entirely on her own, it was quite possible that her father, like many Mexican men, had gone to the States to look for work, and maybe decided to stay there for good. Her mother may well have gone with him. There had to be some explanation for why no one cared whether she spent the night with a stranger in a city nine kilometers from home.

The rain let up and the clouds began to scurry away from a bright full moon. The shadows were long between the slender, moonlit puddles of rain. All the way home in the silvery darkness, I kept an eye out for Estrellita. Any minute, I thought, she could've popped out of the shadows to ask me a silly question: *Why do you live in a big house all alone?* But I didn't see her, and as I approached the depot, the planter was unoccupied. There was no one on the street, only a few scattered cups and potato-chip bags. I stood there for a while, hands in pockets, looking up the dark highway.

ALSO BY POE BALLANTINE

Eighteen-year-old Edgar Donahoe is an orderly at Lemon Acres nursing home. It's not his dream job, but it *is* a surprisingly good place to meet attractive women. In the evenings he lets off steam by drinking beer and popping hallucinogens with his best friend and boon companion, Pat Fillmore. Big, brawling Pat, a Blackfoot Indian, shares Edgar's fondness for drink, drugs and trouble. And trouble is what they get one fateful night when they persuade gentle Beverley, a nurse at the old people's home, to try LSD for the first time.

Set in 1970s California, *God Clobbers Us All* is a wickedly funny coming-of-age story about a young dreamer who loses himself in big waves and escapades. At the same time, it is a thoughtful meditation on the way in which people live and die; a novel that asks why some lives are full of grand gestures, while others are hardly lived at all.

Please see overleaf for an extract from *God Clobbers Us All*.

1.

Dear Deborah:

The sky was so blue today. I had a nice long walk and bought a lemon cake at Food Basket. Lemon cakes with the powdered sugar always remind me of the four weeks Rodney and I spent in Arlington after Father died. When I learned that your father had passed away when you were fifteen too, and then I read the interview where you compared yourself to a Jersey cow, I knew we could be friends. Well. The marigolds are in bloom. It was so cold this winter I thought they might never come up. Mr. Garringer, one of my patients at the hospital, says you can grow anything in California. It must be true. I watched you again last night in Eternity. *My landlord, Winston, loves that movie too, such a kind man. Once when he came for the rent, he stayed for a few minutes to watch part of* This Gun For Hire. *I don't think much of Veronica Lake, though I do like Alan Ladd. A man's height should not have a bearing on his career. I had the strangest dream last night. It was Jean Harlow again and when I woke up I knew Rodney was here. The ladybugs always stir when he comes. I seem to have thousands now. Perhaps*

*too many, but I can't tell Winston and I must leave the lights off
and the curtains closed or he'd bring the pest man. I've circled all
three of your pictures in the guide for this month. Switzerland must
be wonderful this time of year. I hope you begin to act in films again
soon, as I am unable to see you on Broadway. My best to Peter. I
look forward to talking with you again soon.*

　　Your devoted friend,
　　Beverley Fey

2.

HELEN THE ANSWER WOMAN MARCHES THE HOSPITAL AISLES
sixteen hours a day, stopping only to eat or when a nurse
flags her down for medications. She moves with the steadfast
gait of the mountain hiker, slightly pitched to the left, her
cotton diapers sagging, her head tipped so far over you can
see that one day it will simply fall off. Frequently, the day
aides dress her in the garb of her previous existence, a La
Jolla socialite. Though certain Latin terms have been applied,
her diagnosis remains as much a mystery as her destination.
Her husband, a portrait of intense crestfallen bafflement and
anguish, visits once a week. An educated, affluent, intelligent
woman is one day making plans on the phone for cucumber
sandwiches and Jamaica tea with the Opera Club, and the
next moment she is gibbering obliviously down the aisles
of a convalescent hospital, a load in her drawers. Helen rec-
ognizes no one, not even herself. I usually put her to bed

last, so she will be good and tired and not inclined to climb out and resume her march.

At 9pm I find her chattering at Beverley Fey in the ward at the west end of the hospital. Bev, thirty-seven, is a recluse, the original Lemon Acres Nurse's Aide. The number on her time clock actually reads 01. Pocked, thick, and anteater-faced, with a slight limp, I imagine she must have had a horrible disease as a child. Her chopped, reddish, bouffant hair appears to be self-cut with scissors. Though perpetually embarrassed and eager to fade into the woodwork, Bev is the consummate aide. If the hospital held an Employee of the Month competition, it would have a wall full of Beverley Fey photos. She wears a white, severely starched ankle-length uniform dress with the kind of clunky white highly polished thick-soled shoes you would expect to see on a polio victim. Though her forearms are broad, she is still stronger than she looks. She is holding Mr. Sinelfi, a disabled stroke patient whom we call Mr. Logy because he produces a gallon or more of mucus a day, in the air with one arm while she straightens his sheepskin.

Helen babbles at Bev with her head tipped over and her slight mustache twitching. Most of her word parts are composed of the sound *fur*. 'Fur-in-fur,' she says to Bev, hands on hips. 'Fur-furfee-dee-fur.'

Bev smiles at Helen, sets Mr. Logy down, dabs his lips with a washcloth, folds the sheet crisply back over his chest, and produces a cookie from her pocket.

Helen accepts the portion-control institutional Chips

Ahoy package and stares at it as if it were a miniature Phoe-
nician sundial, turning it over in her hands.

'Hello, Bev,' I say.

Bev, startled, turns, pressing palms against thighs. 'Oh,
hello, Edgar. I didn't see you come in.'

'I'm going to need a lasso here pretty soon to catch her,'
I say.

Under that magnificent trunk of a scar-riddled nose, Bev's
wilted rosebud of a mouth breaks into an anguished yellow
smile. She swallows diffidently. Bev is my mother's age. Though
I work practically side by side with her eight hours a night,
four or five times a week, I seldom see her except at parties
afterward, where she will suffer quietly in a corner with
her unfinished glass of wine or Jack and Coke waiting for
someone to drive her home. I don't understand yet Bev's
withdrawal or her Florence Nightingale dedication to her job.
I watch her unwrap Helen's cookie. If Helen were Bev's
patient, I imagine she would be in bed now, snoring tenderly
and dreaming about decaying logarithms or ribbons of Oscar
Mayer smoked ham. Helen begins to munch serenely on her
cookie.

'You forgot to say trick or treat, Helen,' I say. 'How long
has she been here?'

'Oh, just a few minutes. She's all right.' Mr. Logy begins
to cough, working up some good goobers. Bev sops them
up with the damp cloth as they come. Hutchins, the head
nurse, will be in shortly to connect him to a jar so that he
can sleep without drowning.

Bev studies me with her tiny drooping gray eyes and begins to fidget with a thermometer cover. The only way I can ever get her to converse with me is to talk about patients or old movies.

'I saw *From Here to Eternity* last night on KTTV,' I tell her.

The sad gray eyes light. 'So did I,' she says, pouring a glass of water and holding it to Mr. Logy's lips. He seems tranquil now, like a babe in its mother's arms. 'Did you like it?'

I don't want to disappoint Bev, but what can you say about an old movie where the high point is two people smooching in bathing suits on the beach? And there was a commercial every four minutes, *Ralph Williams, Ralph Williams Ford, in the Beautiful City of Encino*... 'It sure was better than the book,' I say. 'I liked the ending.'

'Oh, the ending is wonderful. I must've seen it fifty times.'

'Fifty?'

'Oh, forty or fifty, I don't know. Maybe sixty. As many times as *The King and I*.' She touches her ruffled ostrich hair and her cheeks flush slightly. She seems out of breath with that fluttery enchantment that you only see in her when she talks about her movie stars. 'That was Deborah Kerr's twenty-first movie,' she says, stroking Mr. Logy's head. 'Not counting the first one, *Contraband*, where she got cut out. Joan Crawford was supposed to play Karen Holmes but she didn't like the costumes. Eli Wallach was going to be in it too, but Frank Sinatra got that part. You know the scene where he's shaking the dice? Those are really olives.'

'Olives?'

'Yeah, it was his screen test, but it was so good they just kept it in. Do you know that Deborah got six academy award nominations but never won? That's the most times anyone's ever been nominated without winning.' She shakes her head. 'It isn't fair.'

'I never paid much attention to Deborah Kerr,' I say. 'Is she still alive?'

'She retired from films in 1969. But she's acting on the stage. I think she'll make movies again.'

'You must really admire her.'

'Oh, gosh, yes.' She clasps her big bony hands. 'Have you seen *Black Narcissus* or *The Chalk Garden*?'

'No, I haven't.'

'Oh, you must see them,' she says. 'I have a movie guide…'

Helen has lost interest in her cookie. She seems to want to talk about Deborah Kerr too. 'Fleebie fleebie, doo-fuffy fur,' she offers, enthusiastically.

I have not seen Bev talk this much since I brought up Clark Gable at a party two months ago. I wish I could stay and talk with her. Watching her come to life is like watching the bloom of some rare tropical orchid—but Mr. Logy has begun to gag and now Helen, flagging, has dropped her cookie and turned her attention to me.

'Well, I'd better get her to bed,' I say, retrieving the pieces and pocketing them. 'She'll fall straight over in a minute.'

Bev, suddenly self-conscious, grazes her ear with an index finger. 'Yes, I know.'

'Thanks again for the cookie, Bev.'

'Furfee fur...' says Helen in farewell.

I lead Helen back to her room, which she shares with the Swamp Lady, an insensate skeleton tied to her bedrail to keep her hands out of her faeces. Helen is an easy patient, compliant and eager to converse and please, still the perfect hostess. She babbles all the while I undress her, her eyes seeming to express and understand, her head cocked to the left like a songbird.

I remove her nylons and shoes, shuck her blue-striped dress and brassiere, pitch her diapers in the corner, and sponge the urine from her legs. Helen still has a decent body, firm and flush. I don't believe she has ever had children. She must be in her early fifties. Her feet are lumpy and wide from the thousands of miles she has logged since she landed here in her Fabulous New Realm. We talk about the weather, tropical fish, a weird movie I saw at the Ken Theater recently called *Lemonade Joe*, any subject is all right. I've been feeling filthy and low the last three months. I counsel with her about my mixed-up life:

'It didn't seem wrong when I started...'

'Furdlee-fur.'

'She hates her husband anyway.'

'Hutha-hutha, hur-in-fur,' she answers, eyebrows raised, as if I should've known better from the beginning.

'No need to scold,' I say. 'I know it's wrong. And I'm going to break it off soon, very soon.'

'Oh, sure,' she says.

'I'll tell her tonight. I know you don't believe me, but I will. I just wish I had another girl. Is that too much to ask?'

Helen winces as I scrub her pudendum. I never imagined in my life I would be scrubbing anyone's pudendum. I dust her backside with baby powder. 'Yeeees,' she says. 'Oh, yes. Gleebie-dur-dee-fer-infer.'

'Of course,' I grumble, as I toss the washcloth into the corner with her diapers. 'You're right. But how many billions of women are there in this world, and why can't I just have one I can introduce to my mother and take to the movies and not have to drive out into the boondocks looking in my rearview mirror the whole time to end up on a putting green with?'

'Fer-doodle-dee-der,' she replies confidently.

She wears a grimace as I fasten a fresh pair of diapers over her hips and swaddle her in yellow pajamas with red robins, fat cartoon worms in their beaks. She wriggles and scolds me in her fur language. She may, like a child, simply object to being put to bed, or she may suddenly in some way realize that a strange boy is kneeled before her in her bedroom.

'Are you tired, Helen?' I say.

'Oh, yes,' she croons heartily.

I lead her to bed. 'But you'd also like to walk another forty-three miles.'

'Yes, yes,' she says.

Swamp Lady grunts something from her prehistoric

dreams. She never speaks coherently out of her bearded and withered mouth, though once after I accidentally broke her toe she rose like a vision from the underworld and called me a sonofabitch. I can smell her tarlike faeces, which leak constantly out of her onto a special cotton pad. I pull up Helen's rail. She stares up at the ceiling as if it were bristling with stars. 'Good night, Helen,' I say. 'Good night, Mrs. Swamp...'

3.

AFTER WORK THAT NIGHT, PAT FILLMORE'S TEAL-BLUE MALIBU cruises through the parking lot as I am trying surreptitiously to make extramarital arrangements with Chula La Rue, a twenty-seven-year-old Mexican aide who has three kids.

The window of the Malibu glides down. Pat grins nubby-toothed at me from under her rug of hair cut in the style of a Mongolian rice farmer. Pat and I have been drinking companions for about six months now, ever since she escaped from Montana and became employed as a nurse's aide at Lemon Acres. She is the ruddy, gregarious sort of girl who slams you on the back in greeting and displaces your spine. Her reasons for leaving Montana are unspecified, though she, like so many others flooding into the state, has an obvious California Dream, and once she mentioned standing before a judge who said something to the effect of: *I don't ever want to see you in Bozeman again.*

She nods at me. 'Hey, you horny little wetback,' she says to Chula. 'Bev and I are going out for a drink. You guys wanna come?'

Bev, sitting in three stripes of shadow on the passenger side, looks like a woman behind bars. Whenever I see Pat and Bev together, I think of a large, flaming planet and its distant but enthralled and ice-crusted moon. Bev has always been able to deflect any of our after-work invitations, even the Irresistible Tijuana Martini, but since the arrival of Pat, all of this has changed. Big Pat Fillmore is not the type of person to accept a simple no thank you or two. Hutchins, our skinny, redheaded head nurse, says that while on the surface Pat is trying to help Bev overcome her phobia of society, deep down she is really trying to fix her own loneliness and isolation. Paralyzed by social awkwardness for a good portion of my life, I would like to help Bev break out a little too. 'Where you going?' I say.

'Diablo's,' she answers. 'Then Roberto's for chicken tacos.'

'Sounds good,' I say.

Chula kicks me in the ankle.

'But Chula says something's wrong with her battery. I'm gonna look at it. I think it might be her starter.'

Pat winks at me. She knows I know nothing about cars. 'Maybe you could look at my starter sometime too. Been a while since I had my battery charged.'

I grin amiably, while Chula flips a bored glance up at the stars.

'All RIGHT!' Pat turns up the song on the radio and bellows along with it off-key:

Went to a dance

Lookin' for romance

Saw Bobba-Ran so I pulled down my pants...

'You're coming over tomorrow afternoon with the DICA,' she says, sticking her big round head out the window. In the sodium-vapor lamplight I can almost see the word f-u-n emblazoned in crude gothic DayGlo letters across the upper left quadrant of her soul. 'Right, Eg?'

'Yeah,' I answer nervously. 'I'll bring my battery charger too.'

'Bring-a you DIC-A, honey. That's all I need. Ha! Ha! Hey, I'm gonna tell that one to Doctor Rigatoni. I'll talk to you all tomorrow. Day off! Praise the gourd all Friday! Don't wear off any parts!' Meaty-armed, Pat wrenches the car into drive. The window slides up to the sound of hearty guffaws. I see Bev smiling faintly as the car turns down out of the driveway.

I own a mangy chipped green 1956 Rambler American with surf racks, an oil leak, and an Alpine slide-in stereo I bought on sale at Dow. Chula clambers impatiently into it and says, 'God, when she asked if we wanted to come I almost said, "three times." What the hell is a DICA anyway? You're not screwing her too, are you? I didn't think so. *Chihuahua.* She wouldn't give you your dick back...'

Chula and I drive out to Lake Murray. It is a foggy May Wednesday night, the mist spinning and splashing against the street lamps. I have ended up with Chula not because I wanted to have relations with a married woman but because I found her like a box of free kittens on my front seat one night after a drunken party at Pat's house. We have been going at it for about three months now, and I am looking for a way out. I am not built for the surreptitious, high-pressure intrigue of adultery. I have a plan to go to Australia, which will solve all of my problems in one fell swoop. I have about three hundred bucks in the bank. All I need is a one-way ticket to Perth and I'll hitchhike from there. I am going to build a shack on the beach from fronds and surf and fish all day, eat coconuts or whatever they've got on the beach there in Western Australia. It's going to happen any day.

Chula sits close to me and nibbles my ear. Nurse's aides, in my experience, are the most sexually active group outside of nymphomaniacs, prostitutes, and meat packers. We also party harder per capita than any other occupation, not only because we are poor and our futures are dull, but also because we see every night firsthand the terrible and heartbreaking things that are going to happen to us when we grow old.

I don't know if Chula is a legal citizen. She speaks mildly accented street English sprinkled with Spanish. At the age of twelve, she told me, she came to the United States from deep in jungle Mexico, losing a brother in a sewer tunnel crossing the Texas border. She hustled her way up from the bottom and was lucky in my opinion to find someone dumb enough to marry her. She has no formal education, though she knows how to slaughter and dress a hog. Across her abdomen is a polished blue scar in the shape of an elongated Z, which she alleges came from a boy who raped her with a machete down by the Lacantun River. She uses this story to threaten me, saying that she killed him with the same machete three days later when he was lying on his belly catching turtles: she cut off his head and watched it float away down the river. *You hurt me*, she likes to say, *I hurt you. You cut me, I cut you*. I have my doubts about the veracity of a head floating all by itself down a river. My opinion is that it would sink. Chula is going to be surprised one day when she walks into the lobby of Lemon Acres Convalescent Hospital and finds out that I am gone.

I slow just past the pink stucco restaurant and bait shop on Lake Murray Boulevard, the sign out front reading 'Ten Rolled Tacos for a Dollar,' and turn left onto the dirt road that leads to the lake. I cannot tell if the car that has been following me is her husband's 1964 Galaxie, but I am relieved to see it continue straight along the boulevard. I imagine he will circle back to try to catch us in the act. My sense is that it is not sex these days but the hunt that really excites him. He is an ex-Marine, one of these exceptional few who professes to have enjoyed his tour of duty in Vietnam. Chula is not very attractive anymore, except perhaps to a desperate, sex-crazed, and misguided eighteen-year-old orderly picking up scraps. The gravel pops under my tires as I coast through the gates of the lake.

Chula snuggles into me. She is coffee-skinned, no more than five feet tall, and her teeth are so white that sometimes in the dark they seem blue. She wears her hair teased and pulled back in two tails secured with red rubber bands. Her legs in their dark nylon skins are as hot as link sausages. She has this astounding basal metabolic rate. Her eyes behind black plastic winged specs appear to be charred from the application of excessive mascara. I intend to tell her tonight that we are through, that I have found a girl of my own age and interests. I have made up a name for her: Angelica. Angelica is a timid virgin who lives with her grandparents because her parents were devoured after they fell into the hammerhead tank at Sea World. I drive around to the other side of the lake, glancing in my mirror, and park by the dam. Chula sets her winged specs up on the dashboard.

'Chula?'

'What is it, baby?'

'There's something I need to tell you.'

'Oh, *nene*,' she says. 'Kiss me first before you go on with your philosophical bullshit. I like a boy who shoots first and asks questions later.'

I turn on the radio. Chula intimidates me. I hate being afraid of a woman barely five feet tall. She begins to unzip my fly. I catch headlights dissolving in my rearview mirror. There would be no one out by the lake at this time of the morning, not legitimate fishermen anyway, only killers, drifters, dopers, and jealous husbands.

'Wait a minute ...'

'What is wrong with you tonight, *corazónsillo*?' she says.

'That car behind us.'

'What car?'

'It's him.'

'Who?'

'Your old man.'

'That ain't him,' she scoffs, turning her head listlessly.

'How can you tell?'

'What are you talking about, *hijo*?' she says.

'He's playing a game with us.'

'Mike doesn't play games. If he knew about us he'd be roasting your *huevitos* now with anchos on the barbecue.'

The headlights spring on again, as if cued, and the car creeps out into the road. I cower down in the seat. Chula laughs. 'He's not smart enough to find us,' she says.

'The guy was in *Nam*,' I say.

'Relax. He's asleep. Snoring away like a little pig. He never stays up past the ten o'clock news and his seven Budweisers.'

The car passes. It's too dark to see inside, but Chula's right: it's a station wagon, teens smoking weed or a couple of bottom-fish poachers looking for a spot.

I begin to take off Chula's clothes. Her hair is tough as fishing line. Naked, she smells of gardenias and popcorn and muskrat. Before I know it we are down on the seat, fogging up the windows. The ripple waves of the black and mist-locked lake below slush up and back through the pebbled shore. In the cup of Chula's throat I concentrate on a little Catholic medal glittering on a chain. I hear a car go by. I don't look up, but I know it has to be him.